T0114810

FROSTY WOOLDRIDGE

AMERICA'S OVERPOPULATION PREDICAMENT:
Blindsiding Future Generations

authorHOUSE

AuthorHouse™
1663 Liberty Drive
Bloomington, IN 47403
www.authorhouse.com
Phone: 833-262-8899

Published by AuthorHouse 03/01/2021

ISBN: 978-1-6655-1782-9 (sc)
ISBN: 978-1-6655-1781-2 (e)

Library of Congress Control Number: 2021903976

Print information available on the last page.

This book is printed on acid-free paper.

Dedicated to Sandi Lynn Wooldridge for her steadfast support, inspiration, editing and encouragement over the years. Her sparkling countenance, wicked wit and amazing charm make my days at this "keyboard salt mine" much better emotionally, mentally and spiritually. Her radiant smile and dancing eyes forever envelop me in that most delicious of life's treasures: love. Thank you, Sandi, for every moment on our adventure through life, together. You make it one whale of a magical ride!

CONTENTS

SECTION 1 THE DEADLIEST BIRTH RATE AFFECTING ALL HUMANITY

SECTION 2 WHAT OUR CIVILIZATION FACES: IT'S THE LITTLE
THINGS THAT ADD UP TO BIG PROBLEMS

SECTION 3 ENVIRONMENTAL, SOCIOLOGICAL, QUALITY OF LIFE ISSUES

SECTION 4 COMPELLING REASONS TO CHANGE COURSE

SECTION 5 ODDS, ENDS AND SOLUTIONS

SECTION 6 ACTIONS AND SOLUTIONS

INTRODUCTION

///

"The apocalypse didn't happen overnight. The world didn't end in a satisfying climax of explosive special effects. It was slow. It was boring. It was one little thing at a time. One building here another factory over there. [One plastic container tossed into the ocean and then another and another until their numbers reached 5.25 trillion floating or sunk beneath the waves.] One moral compromise, one abandoned ideal, and one more justified injustice. No dramatic wave of destruction sweeping across the world, just scattered spots of rot forming throughout the decades, seemingly isolated incidents until the moment they all **merged**." Isaac Marion, **The Burning World**

One of my readers said, "What you've written is like a "Parade of Horribles" because it *is* a parade of "horribles." And you are correct! If humanity doesn't solve it, Mother Nature will respond brutally by no longer providing the resources to feed us. She will offer pandemic diseases we've never seen before. Either way, we're doing irreparable damage to the planet, and at some point, this planet will respond."

Another reader said, "Your book is freaking scary! What's worse is that it's supported by scientific and observable facts. You've masterfully put together a story that no one wants to pay attention to, but a future that will affect everyone on this planet. No matter who you are, you cannot deny the negative impact of human numbers. We've created a "monster civilization" of 330 million people that cannot be sustained. The roots appear to be traced to our insatiable appetite for growth...and an attitude of damn the costs. Consumerism! How do you tell people to turn off desire for bigger, faster, newer and fancier? Maybe the planet has the answer. Screw with Mother Nature long enough and she'll screw you back twice as hard. I predict "The Next Big One"—as in climate change, will thin our ranks. I'm personally frightened."

Another reader said, "What does 'blindsiding' mean?"

To clarify, in hockey, if a player skates down the ice and the 'enforcer' hits him from behind, it's called a 'blindside hit' because the victim didn't see it coming. In professional football, an illegal block in the back is also a 'blindside hit'. The victim didn't see it coming. In the title of this book, our children heading toward 2050, don't have a clue as to what's coming as to human overpopulation. They are being 'blindsided' by the baby boomer generation that did little to nothing to stop the consequences of overpopulation. I would add that America's mainstream media kept the American people in the dark since Earth Day 1970. They have been avoiding and suppressing the overpopulation topic at every juncture. Why, I don't know, because their kids will be embroiled in the consequences, too. Every person and animal on the planet faces being 'blindsided' in the coming years. Their fate will become painfully apparent as you read this book.

The Underlying Problem

When I lived and worked in Antarctica as a journalist from 1997 to 1998, top climate scientists filled my notebooks with foreboding facts. Our massive "carbon footprint" from 7.8 billion humans burning fossil fuels 24/7—would ultimately create "catastrophic climate destabilization." That phenomenon also goes by "climate change" and, "global warming." I wrote about it, but much like today, everyone avoided it. Unfortunately, few want to tie it to human overpopulation—its main driver.

"It's important for me to have hope because that's my job as a parent, to have hope for my kids, that we're not going to leave them in a world that's in shambles, that's a chaotic place, that's a dangerous place." James Cameron, Film Director, Titanic

What you will read in this book provides you with a clarion call by some of the finest minds on this planet, both in the past and in the present. Many Nobel Laureates speak on these pages. All of them bring their lifetimes of scientific evidence, personal experiences and common sense to the reality facing every single American. That includes every human being on the planet of every race, creed, color and economic class. No matter how smart you might be, or educated, or wealthy—like the Titanic, we're all passengers on the same ship.

Have you heard of the Faustian Bargain? It means that the top corporate money-makers push for more people, production, consumption and profits to fund their lavish lifestyles today—with no concern for the future. Yet, the future gallops toward humanity at breakneck speed. When you multiply those thousands of corporations planet-wide, along with 7.8 billion people, and headed toward 10 billion, refer back to Isaac Marion's quote…when all the consequences **"merged."**

Today, the Faustian Bargain manifests daily in America as we "grew" the stock exchange to over 30,000 points in November 2020. The higher those numbers climb, the more damage to our planet. Why? Because corporate economic success comes at the expense of the Natural World. Each time the markets advance, the Natural World gets hit with extractions from its non-renewable natural resources. Every day we add another 240,000 babies, net gain around the planet, and nearly 1.0 million more babies every four days. With an additional 83 million people annually, the planet staggers under the onslaught. Earth bends to the "Tragedy of the Commons" as explained in Chapter 27.

At some point in the next 29 years, the energy-driver that allowed humans to jump from 3.5 billion in 1970 during Earth Day, to 7.8 billion in 2021, will be exhausted: **oil!** Here is what you can expect:

"As we go from this happy hydrocarbon bubble, we have reached now to a renewable energy resource economy, which we do this century, will the "civil" part of civilization survive? As we both know there is no way that alternative energy sources can supply the amount of per capita energy we enjoy now, much less for the 10 billion expected by 2050. And energy is what keeps this game going. We are involved in a Faustian bargain— selling our economic souls for the luxurious life of the moment, but sooner or later the price has to be paid." Walter Youngquist, **Geodestinies**

As Youngquist noted, we disregarded the red blinking warning lights on the dashboard in 1970 to add another 4.3 billion of ourselves to reach 7.8 billion in 2021. Who thought that was a good idea? Why didn't world leaders organize conferences to address the most important issue facing humanity back in 1970 and still haven't in 2021? Why did countries like India, China, Mexico, Bangladesh, Egypt, Pakistan or the entire continent of Africa think they could accelerate those kinds of population gains without consequences? What happened to them? Answer: relentless poverty, species extinctions, catastrophic climate destabilization, degraded quality of life and escalating damage to Earth's eco-systems. The United Nations states that 1.5 to 2.0 billion people live in misery:

"Around 1.89 billion people, or nearly 36 percent of the world's population, live in extreme poverty. Nearly half the population in developing countries lives on less than $1.25 a day." (Source: www.worldvision.org)

At the same time, we humans burn nearly 100 million barrels of oil 24/7. By 2050, experts project 200 million barrels of oil will be burned daily.

The Energy Information Administration (EIA) estimated that the world consumed 97 million barrels per day in 2017, with the top 10 consumers accounting for 60 percent of the total consumption.

The U.S. Energy Information Administration estimated that in 2019, the United States emitted 5.1 billion metric tons of energy-related carbon dioxide, while the global emissions of energy-related carbon dioxide totaled 32.5 billion metric tons.

Are these numbers significant? How do you think this planet responds to that kind of abuse? As the world's oceans warm-up from ingesting massive amounts of CO_2, they magnify normal hurricanes into "monster" hurricanes like Katrina, Sandy, Irvine and dozens more bashing down our coastlines. What about Washington State, Oregon, California, Montana and Colorado enduring millions of acres on fire each summer? What about "exceptional" droughts now gripping most of Western America? Don't forget Florida's water shortages! (Source: The highest category, **exceptional drought**, or D4, corresponds to an area experiencing **exceptional** and widespread forest, crop and pasture losses, fire risk, and water shortages that result in water emergencies. This is part of a series of articles about monitoring and assessing drought conditions across the United States. www.ncdc.noaa.gov)

In 2018, when I bicycled the entire West Coast of America, a newspaper report gave a figure of 12 million trees had died the year before from lack of water. I witnessed it firsthand because everywhere, brown, dead grass dominated the landscape. Their exceptional drought conditions caused enormous wildfires, while at the same time, the entire ecology of the land changed drastically. So much so, the environment of the area moved more toward desert conditions where native California animals could not survive. Because of "catastrophic climate destabilization", it's possible that we could lose those 2,500 year old redwoods at some future date because they won't be able to pull enough water from dry soils.

Despite all these realities, we Americans continue adding millions and millions of refugees from around the world onto our shores. **Those immigrants add 35 million, net gain, to our population every decade.**

Why do you think they flee their own countries? Answer: China, India, Mexico, Somalia, Congo and numerous other countries cannot feed, water or educate their added 83 million babies annually.

In reality, it's greater than 83 million new babies, net gain, annually. I've added the following paragraph to clarify that what's happening to developing countries, will soon occur to all Western countries as to immigration as a safety valve for all other overpopulated countries.

Each year, 60 million humans die of all causes.(2) (Source: www. ourworldindata.org) The developing world not only adds another 60 million new babies, but 83 million more on top of that. That's a total of 143 million new babies that need to be fed, watered, housed, educated and new jobs created. Guess what? Those countries cannot do it. That's why illiteracy and more babies expect to increase the human population to 10 billion, give or take a few million by 2050. (Source: United Nations Population Projections, 2017)

And what about our oceans? How do you think they are surviving with 5.25 trillion pieces of plastic floating on the surface or sunk beneath the waves? Are you aware that we humans add 8.0 million more pieces of plastic 24/7 because there aren't any effective national-international deposit-return laws? (3) Can you imagine the deaths and destroyed eco-systems of the planet's marine life? We're talking into the millions upon millions, which in turn become extinction rates.

What about 84,000 chemicals that end up in the oceans? How's that going to turn out? For starters, marine biologists report on severe destruction of reefs worldwide. Additionally, entire marine breeding and birthing sanctuaries suffer contamination from chemicals injected into "dead zones." According to the latest reports on the "Sixth Extinction Session"— we lose 24 to 100 species to extinction every day of the year. That's both on land and in the oceans!

In this introduction, I've covered the bare bones. While everything "looks" okay today in America, Canada, Europe and Australia—all Western civilizations face a destructive "riptide" under the surface. That riptide will become more deadly for all of us in the next 29 years. What you will read in the forthcoming chapters will sober you, and perhaps distress you!

Why? Because your children will inherit this mess. They will be blindsided like no other generation in the history of humanity. Young people like the Swedish student Greta Thunberg and University of Miami graduate Adam Roberti know it's coming. Some adults mock them from the comfort of their lounge chairs while pushing their remote to the next sitcom. Nonetheless, those young activists speak out passionately, but at the same time, the world's adults hold onto power, thus maintaining the status quo. Which translates into "doing very little" as to helping this planet's ability to regain its equilibrium.

After reading this sobering book, you will either choose to do nothing or you will choose to take action. If we're going to salvage our civilization, we need to take action. You will find the last three chapters offer you ample guidance. You may use your skills and talents to become involved on multiple levels. Hint, most people feel too hopeless and helpless to get involved. My suggestion: think of your own heroes and what they faced. Did they give up?

If not for the fortitude of John Muir, we wouldn't enjoy National Parks to experience for all time. If not for Susan B. Anthony, women still wouldn't be allowed to vote. If not for Martin Luther King, we wouldn't have equal rights and voting power for people of color. If not for Dwight D. Eisenhower, we wouldn't have liberated Europe. If not for Amelia Earhart, women wouldn't be flying F-16 fighter jets. Each in their own time overcame doubt and huge obstacles—yet they triumphed. This is your time, your moment, your chance. You may not become famous; however, you will make a huge difference in the viability of our civilization and your children's lives.

My goal: I intend to create a national-international annual conference of world leaders, environmentalists, population experts, religious leaders and climate specialists to discuss-debate solutions to our overpopulation dilemma. We need to accelerate production of alternative energy. We need to discuss one child per woman birthrates via education and personal choice. And, we need to discuss related ideas to gracefully bring human numbers in line with the finite carrying capacity of this planet. While this conference would ideally be funded by an international consortium of nations, it may need to be privately funded because you won't see our government officials ever doing anything to pull us out of this mess.

Additionally, I advise each city and state to pass legislation on a: "U.S. Sustainable Population Policy...U.S. Carrying Capacity Policy...U.S. Quality of Life Policy...U.S. Ecological Footprint Policy...U.S. Sustainable Resources Policy."

My other goals include interviews with top population-climate-environmental experts concerning overpopulation on 60 Minutes, NPR, PBS, Meet the Press, Face the Nation, Talk of the Nation, and countless audiences to view my program: *The Coming Overpopulation Crisis Facing America: and how to change course.* I intend to speak to a joint-session of Congress to educate them as to what all of our children face.

Additionally, I have provided fact checks within the copy for immediate verification. Additionally, you will see (1) (2) (3).... for footnote support data in the Index of this book. Everything I've written in this book is supported by verifiable facts. When you see repetition throughout the book, I'm attempting to show you the enormity of our situation. I want these facts to stick in your head.

Finally, I want you to understand this book doesn't mince facts or our harsh realities. We humans stand eyeball deep in trouble. If we don't solve the "catastrophic climate destabilization" or "plasticized oceans" or "species extinction rates" or "collapse of pollinators" or the "human overpopulation equation" within the next 10 years—it's very possible if not probable that this planet will violently and methodically "backwash" on the human species as well as the rest of our fellow Earth travelers. That's you and me. The planet won't care if you are religious or atheist, black, white or brown, liberal or conservative, care or don't care and another ten variables you might choose. Worst of all, it's your children who will be facing Earth's wrath.

Your goal: after digesting the information in this book, you're invited to take action at the local, state and national levels. If you are a citizen of a Western country, please organize groups of like-minded people to drive this issue to the highest levels in your country. You may utilize the last three chapters to take action.

Understand this reality: like the Titanic, we continue speeding toward the population iceberg. Everyone on board will be harshly affected, even the survivors. On a personal level, we're all like Thelma & Louise driving that 1966 Thunderbird over a cliff. Is that what you want for your children? Because if you don't, the key word to urgent change is "action" in your community, city, state and this nation.

Let's get started!

THE PERFECT STORM GATHERING OVER AMERICA!

"We must alert and organize the world's people to pressure world leaders to take specific steps to solve the two root causes of our environmental crises – exploding population growth and extreme consumption of irreplaceable resources. Overpopulation underlies every environmental problem we face today." Jacques-Yves Cousteau, Oceanographer

Right now, America gallops toward a demographic cliff with the intensity of a Kentucky Derby racehorse. Americans watch their country expand on average 3.1 million annually. (4) In reality, we also add another 500,000 people annually from illegal immigration. U.S. Census Bureau projections show the United States accelerating from 300 million in 2006 to a mind-numbing 439 million by 2050. (Source: U.S. Census Bureau, www.cis.org, www.PewResearchCenter.org, Fogel/Martin "U.S. Population Projections.")

The research of an increasing number of global resource experts, including the extensive data of Global Footprint Network, (https://www.footprintnetwork.org/), verifies that current human numbers, both globally and in the U.S., surge alarmingly above the *sustainable* levels that our renewable resources can support. On this finite planet, non-renewable natural resources can sustain less than 1.0 billion people—dramatically less than our current 7.8 billion! The levels of consumption and pollution from those 1.0 billion people must become significantly lower than the current unsustainable levels of average Americans. Research shows that a sustainable U.S. population ranges well under 100 million. (5) (Dr. Jack Alpert, www.skil.org)

While Americans squirm daily in gridlocked traffic in every major city in our country, they fail to connect the dots as to the long-term ramifications of adding 100 million more people to the equation in the next 29 years—in our already overpopulated country.

How do you put 100 million more people into context? Answer: adding that many people equates to doubling the human population of our 35 most populated cities. In some cases, it means doubling the population of entire states. For example, New York City-Newark houses 18 million people today. That metropolitan area would double to 36 million. Los Angeles at 11 million expects to exceed 22 million—and on down the line for 33 other cities. States like Florida remain on track to grow from 21.5 million to 33 million in three decades. None of these projections need occur! We must change course!

But like those people fuming in traffic as they breathe their own fumes, few of them connect the dots. If your car's dashboard warning lights flash to red, you stop your car to check for low oil, leaking radiator fluid or a leaking transmission case.

Today, planet Earth's dashboard lights flash red with countless warnings. As humans burn 99 million barrels of oil worldwide 24/7, we exhaust billions of tons of carbon into the atmosphere that ultimately dumps into the oceans, warming them. That warming and acidification of ocean waters causes the deaths of entire ecological systems like reefs and fish spawning grounds. It's also causing our polar ice caps to melt, which, in turn, forces the oceans to rise. By the middle to the end of this century, we will see massive flooding of our coastlines and our cities engulfed.

According to the Norman Myers 40-year study at Oxford University, an average of 24 to 100 species suffer extinction 24/7 around the globe. Most of it via human encroachment, but more expected by climate change because those animals cannot adapt quickly enough to changing temperatures in their habitats. (6) (Source: wwf.panda.org)

That same warming trend causes "catastrophic climate destabilization" which magnifies hurricanes like Harvey, Sandy and Katrina.

How much oil do we burn that dumps that much carbon into our oceans? To give you an idea, an oil drum holds 42 gallons. It's 20 inches in diameter across the bottom of the drum. If you take 99 million drums of oil and stand them side-by-side, they create a belt of oil in excess of 25,000 miles around the equator. We fill them up at midnight and burn them down to empty 24/7. The biosphere cannot continue such relentless abuse. I learned these realities when I worked with top climate scientists in Antarctica in 1997-1998.

Nobel Laureate Dr. Henry W. Kendall said, **"If we don't halt population growth with justice and compassion, it will be done for us by nature, brutally and without pity – and will leave a ravaged world."**

What did he mean by that stark statement?

As a world bicycle traveler across six continents, I witnessed firsthand Dr. Kendall's statement. One look at China and India gives you an idea of the consequences of overpopulation at its end-most destination. For example, Bangladesh houses 161 million people in a landmass less than the size of the State of Iowa. Can you imagine half the U.S. population living in Iowa? Can you fathom the ecological damage as to shortages of drinkable water, sewage effluence, carbon emission exhausts, and difficulty of growing food to nourish 161 million impoverished bodies, not to mention human crowding and lack of any quality of life? Tragically, Bangladesh accelerates toward 201 million people by 2050. Why are they choosing that kind of a future for their country? Who in their right mind would want that kind of a grim, science fiction future for America?

To give you an idea of what the United States faces, we increase our own population along the same path as those ancient countries.

We Americans continue on course to double our population of 330 million in 2021 to 625 million by the end of this century, a scant 79 years from now. This is well within the lifetimes of our children born today. This 10-minute video by Roy Beck of www.NumbersUSA.com shows America's end point in the 21st century: (You can access it at that website titled: **Immigration Off the Charts**, or this link.)

http://www.youtube.com/watch?v=muw22wTePqQ

Did you swallow hard by watching Roy Beck's video as to what your children face? What do these facts mean to our water, energy, arable land, food and resources—in a country that's already over-consuming, over-polluting and overpopulated? What about our quality of life and standard of living? What about our wilderness areas and the animals and plants that share North America with us?

Let's examine our water as the most important resource for living on this planet. We need to drink it, water our livestock and irrigate our crops. Yet today, seven states face imminent water shortages: Florida, Georgia, Texas, New Mexico, Arizona, Nevada, and California. Today, with severe water shortages, California, boasting 39 million people, remains on track to add 15 to 20 million more people by 2050. Does anyone with a brain think that's going to work out for everyone?

Florida suffers stark water shortfalls with 21.5 million people, yet projections show 33 million people by 2050.

Oil energy drives America's entire society. Without it, no amount of wind, solar or nuclear energy can propel this society into the future. Unfortunately, we import seven out of 10 barrels of the 19 million barrels of oil we burn 24/7. Yes, we are "fracking" for the last remnants of oil in North America, but that "last resort" drilling will run dry very quickly.

Don't you find it astounding that none of our elected leaders even mentions anything about what we face when "Peak Oil" depletes our supplies and all other supplies on this planet?

From my own research, at current rates of resource consumption, we can safely calculate that both fossil fuels *(**mostly gone by 2040-50**)* and industrial materials (non-renewable natural resources) will be fully or mostly depleted for all practical purposes in less than 29 years. Our economic systems, and our global factories along with farms will come to a screeching halt. (Refer to resources being exhausted in Chapter 22.)

No inputs = No outputs. No outputs = No Survival

Author Christopher Clugston, in 2012, wrote the book, **Scarcity: Humanity's Final Chapter. The realities, choices and outcomes associated with ever-increasing non-renewable natural resource scarcity.** He highlighted the 80 most critical metals and minerals essential to all modern societies. We require lead, zinc, cadmium, copper and more to create products such as batteries, cars, glass, metals and other vital products that make our civilization operate. We face exhaustion of the Earth's stores of those precious non-renewable resources by mid-21st century. Once NRR's are depleted, as Porky Pig said, "That's all folks!"

In 2020, Clugston wrote a second book that defined our chances of survival in the 21st century, **Blip: Humanity's Self-Terminating Experiment with Industrialism.** "What we do to enable our existence simultaneously undermines our existence. Our persistent and ever-increasing extraction and utilization of NNR's (non-renewable natural resources)—the finite and non-replenishing fossil fuels, metals and nonmetallic minerals that enable our industrial existence—is causing increasingly pervasive global NNR scarcity. This, in turn, is causing faltering global human prosperity, which is causing increasing global political instability, economic fragility and societal unrest. This scenario will intensify during the coming decades and culminate in humanity's permanent global societal collapse, almost certainly by the year 2050."

Clugston doesn't make these predictions lightly or even based on only his research. He synthesizes the quantitative and qualitative evidence produced by hundreds of scientists, scholars, researchers and analysts in the various physical sciences and behavioral sciences that address the origins and evolution of industrial humanity and human industrialism. Those experts produced the "dots" which Clugston connected clearly and comprehensibly in **Blip.** If you didn't catch the term "blip" correctly, it means we've only worked the Industrial Revolution for 300 years…a "blip" in time. But now, we're coming to the end of it…rather abruptly.

After I talked to Mr. Clugston, he told me that it might be ironic that I am encouraging Americans to take action today to prepare for that ominous date of 2050 when all the NNR's will be exhausted. In other words, it will be too late, and in fact, it's probably already too late. Because, even if the United States attempted to reduce NNR usage as well as begin massive recycling programs, it would not help because the rest of the world's economies will gallop merrily toward their own mid-century nightmares. If we take action NOW, we might enjoy an inkling of a chance to survive what's coming.

At the same time, we Americans don't think about the ramifications of adding 3.1 million people annually to our already overpopulated civilization. (We add another 500,000 illegally, as well as their birthrates.) However, the Natural World takes the brunt of the damage.

Twenty years ago, Oprah Winfrey alerted the world about the "Great Pacific Garbage Patch" located 1,000 miles off the coast of San Francisco. Swirling between two ocean gyres and 30 to 60 feet deep, it features 100 million tons, and some 5.25 trillion pieces of floating plastics of every description from Bic lighters to soda pop containers to toothbrushes to Styrofoam—in an area the size of Texas. Millions of marine and avian lives suffer death annually after consuming or becoming entangled in plastic. Micro particles of plastic now inhabit the tissue of fish that humans eat.

It's so serious that today, scientists have discovered plastic in the fetuses of babies. The reporter said, "The oceans which are the womb of Mother Earth are filled with plastics. Now, the wombs of mothers are filled with micro-plastics." (Source: www.wion.com, December 25, 2020.)

https://www.facebook.com/WIONews/videos/226374932197635

Once the Garbage Patch was discovered, did the world respond with a 50-cent deposit-return law internationally to give incentives to recycle all forms of plastic? No! In fact, since that report, the "patch" grew from 60 million tons of plastic to its current 100 million tons.

Oceanographer experts like Julia Whitty of **Onearth Magazine** explained that humans toss 8.0 million more plastic containers as well as other plastics into the oceans 24/7. Her findings show that, on average, 46,000 plastic containers float on every square mile of our oceans. Trust me, as a lifelong scuba diver, I know these numbers are hard to comprehend, but they are well-researched from multiple sources. That same report showed 100,000,000 sharks being killed by humans annually, since 1990. If continued, many shark species face extinction. (7) (Source: **Life Magazine**, August 1991, "Shark Alert! The age-old struggle between man and shark has become a killing frenzy. We are slaughtering 100 million every year, driving them to extinction.")

"Upwards of one hundred species, mostly of the large, slow-breeding variety, are becoming extinct here every day

because more and more of the earth's carrying capacity is systematically being converted into human carrying capacity. These species are being burnt out, starved out, and squeezed out of existence, thanks to technologies that most people think of as technologies of peace." Daniel Quinn

Let that quote sink into your mind and heart: "...more and more of earth's carrying capacity is systematically being converted into human carrying capacity." In what system of morality can humans allow this endless destruction of life to occur? And why? To what end?

What do we face in America with another 100 million people by 2050 as to species extinction rates? Have you heard the term "ecological footprint?" It's never discussed by leaders or the media. They avoid any mention of the dark underbelly of human overpopulation in America. It's always "Out there in the developing world."

For example: a person living in Ethiopia, Africa utilizes .4 acres of land or 4/10ths of an acre to build a dwelling, grow food and live. When such a person emigrates to America, his or her ecological footprint explodes to 25.4 acres. (Source: www. AllSpecies.org, "Ecological Footprint") When you multiply 25.4 acres X's 100,000,000 added people to the USA, that equates to 2.54 **billion acres** of wilderness that must be destroyed for housing, malls, roads, schools and more. Where do the animals go? They go extinct!

In my worldwide bicycle travels, I've seen human misery on a scale most Americans cannot comprehend. While traveling through China, I saw 50 lanes of gridlocked highways. (You read correctly: 50 lanes!) I witnessed air pollution thicker than the boiler room on the Titanic. I observed people and housing thicker than hair on a dog. I saw wilderness desecration beyond repair. I floated on the Yangtze River which resembled an open sewer creating a 20,000 square mile dead zone at its mouth.

This video link depicts fifty lanes of traffic gridlocked in China:
(https://www.youtube.com/watch?v=MJKN1LzVakA)

When it comes to quality of life or standard of living, countries like China at 1.4 billion and India at 1.3 billion, cannot correct their population calamities. While it proved too late, China instituted a one-child per woman policy across the country in 1979. It may be harsh, but Mother Nature proves merciless and much more brutal with her methods.

One look at India's population overshoot shows a full 60 percent of Indians do not enjoy access to a toilet. (Source: Indian Express Newspaper, November 19, 2015, "India has 60.4 per cent people without access to toilet.") They add 14 million people, net gain, annually! Having swallowed the beast, India now suffers major population indigestion.

Since American women averaged 2.03 children since 1970, our country would have leveled out at 255 million in 1990. (8) Instead, we screamed past 300 million by 2006. Question: what drives our population to such horrific numbers? Answer: the 1965 Immigration Reform Act passed by Congress forced constant immigration of 1.1 to 1.5 million annually, along with 900,000 births annually by immigrants, and fueled endless chain-migration. That equates to 2.0 million and more annually, plus our own population momentum of 1.0 million annually. (Source: Dr. Steven Camarota, www.cis.org)

In his brilliant book, **Unguarded Gates**, Dr. Otis Graham said, *"Most Western elites continue urging the wealthy West not to stem the migrant tide [that adds 80 million new babies net gain annually to the planet], but to absorb our global brothers and sisters until their horrid ordeal has been endured and shared by all—ten billion humans packed onto an ecologically devastated planet."*

In the end, what about Mother Nature and all the animals? How can a cognitive species such as humans with so much power over this planet, eradicate countless other species without a touch of moral culpability?

America's first ecologist in the 1800's, John Muir said, *"How many hearts with warm red blood in them are beating under the cover of the woods, and how many teeth and eyes are shining! A multitude of animal people, intimately related to us, but of whose lives we know almost nothing, are as busy about their own affairs as we are about ours."*

Instead of continuing on this "exponential growth" path, the same modus operandi of a cancer cell, a national discussion on the future of our country grows more critical by the hour. Do we want a successful future for our children or one like India's, China's and Mexico's?

Such a national discussion must generate an international debate on why the entire human race continues stumbling, staggering and procreating into the 21st century.

If you were a child today, would you want your parents to avoid this discussion? Would you want them to let you become a victim of this overpopulation juggernaut? Would you like to be swimming inside a human caldron of 439 million people surging toward 625 million in the span of a lifetime of a child born today? (9) (Source: US expected to reach 625 million within 79 years, www.NumbersUSA.org)

We live in a Constitutional Republic. Nothing happens unless we, the citizens, speak up, write up and stand up. Let's force a national discussion onto every radio, TV and cable channel. Let's write every newspaper and magazine that discusses our national interests. Let's speak to the producers of "60 Minutes", NPR, CBS, NBC, ABC, FOX, CNN and PBS. Let's speak on "Meet the Press" and "Face the Nation."

My late friend and distinguished professor of physics at the University of Colorado, Dr. Albert Bartlett, dedicated his life to educating millions about the dangers of human overpopulation. ("Arithmetic, Population, and Energy" www.albartlett.org) You may access his presentation at:

www.youtube.com/watch?v=O133ppiVnWY

Bartlett said, **"Unlimited population growth cannot be sustained; you cannot sustain growth in the rates of consumption of resources. No species can overrun the carrying capacity of a finite land mass. This Law cannot be repealed and is not negotiable."**

Human overpopulation, nationally and globally, must be solved! Otherwise, we humans face Mother Nature for our final destiny. It's already occurring. The United Nations reports 4.1 million children starve to death annually as well as 8.0 million adult deaths from extreme poverty. Two billion humans struggle to survive, daily! Another 165 million children scrape to survive with stunted bodies and minds because of malnutrition. **Freedom from Hunger** states, "Sixty-six million primary school-age children attend classes hungry across the developing world." (Source: www.freedomfromhunger.org)

The 1984 movie "Terminator," starring Arnold Schwarzenegger, illustrated the human overpopulation crisis perfectly. In the movie, this dialogue occurred in the car as Sara Connor bites Kyle's hand after he rescues her from the night club...Kyle said, "Cyborgs don't feel pain. I do. Don't do that again."

Sarah said, "Just let me go!"

Kyle said, "Listen and understand! That terminator is out there. It can't be bargained with. It can't be reasoned with. It doesn't feel pity, or remorse, or fear. And it will absolutely not stop, ever, until you are dead."

That's what human overpopulation is, a "Terminator." It doesn't care about your feelings, religion, status, age or condition. It cares nothing about your family, community, country or environment. It is an equal opportunity extinction machine.

Another note: you will hear about "wonderful" progress in green energy production by power companies. They tout wind turbines, solar panels, wave and nuclear energy. Unfortunately, they facilitate greater incentives to grow human populations that overwhelm the Natural World.

How can we save ourselves? Answer: we must graciously and equitably reduce birthrates worldwide via birth control, including the U.S., and we must greatly restrict immigration into our country and all Western countries. **Help those citizens in their own countries.**

Ironically, developing countries add 83 million people, net gain, annually. Here's why we must help them in their own countries via Roy Beck, "Immigration, Gumballs, and Poverty." You can access it off his website: www.NumbersUSA.org

http://www.youtube.com/watch?v=LPjzfGChGlE&feature=player embedded

We must reduce America's population slowly and effectively to under 100 million people, i.e., gracefully with birth control. This could be possible within two to three generations and bring with it a sustainable standard of living roughly equal to that which Americans enjoy today.

Additionally, we must engage a strict incentive-driven recycling of all products, i.e., paper, plastics, glass, metals and everything produced by humanity. We must recover our oceans. We must stop poisoning everything and everyone around the globe. That means we must terminate Monsanto, Bayer and Dow Chemical from their continued injections of deadly chemicals like Roundup, Weed-B-Gone and hundreds of herbicides and pesticides.

As citizens concerned about what we bequeath to future generations, I can't imagine anyone wanting to see our (your) children struggling for water, food and energy in an overpopulated America, or the world.

Only by these humane and reasoned choices can we avoid greater misery, suffering and environmental breakdown across the U.S. and the globe.

Personally, I would like to bequeath to future generations a vibrant, green, thriving and healthy planet. Each child deserves to drink clean water, run through fresh air, eat nourishing poison-free, non-GMO foods and move toward his or her own meaningful life.

Let's move toward John Muir's legacy:

"Camp out among the grass and gentians of glacier meadows, in craggy garden nooks full of Nature's darlings. Climb the mountains and enjoy their good tidings. Nature's peace will flow into you as sunshine flows into trees. The winds will blow their own freshness into you, and the storms their energy, while cares will drop off like autumn leaves."

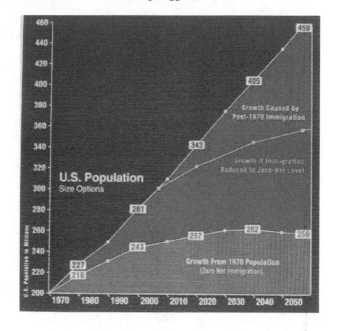

(This population graph shows our upward growth toward 439 million by 2050.)

CAN WE OR WILL WE SAVE OURSELVES
FROM EXPONENTIAL GROWTH?

The mantra of continuous growth in America echoes from every mayor, governor, senator, House member—all the way to the president of the United States. Every CEO, principal, store owner, car dealership, movie theater owner, fast food joint, hardware store, well, just about every business—demands, expects and gains from exponential growth of human population. Main driver: profits and wealth!

The late Dr. Albert Bartlett, physics professor at the University of Colorado, warned that exponential growth remained the modus operandi of a cancer cell. Ultimately, the cancer cells kill the host body by multiplying beyond the host body's ability to sustain them.

Additionally, he said, "Anyone who believes or promotes exponential growth may be termed an innumerate. What does that mean? It means that person is mathematically illiterate."

He attempted to show people with his one-hour slide show that continuous growth ultimately leads to collapse of any society.

Jared Diamond in his book, **Collapse: How Societies Choose to Fail or Succeed**, illustrated Bartlett's point by researching failed societies throughout history. Every one of them that followed exponential growth—crashed. **The great civilizations of China, India and others will see their own collapse in the 21st century. They will disintegrate from lack of water, energy, arable land for crops and resources.** Additionally, all overloaded countries and their cities face horrific environmental decay and degradation. If you look at quality of life and standard of living, as the human numbers accelerate, both aspects plummet downward in a vertical line of human misery.

Can the United States, Canada, Australia and Europe save themselves? That's for each country to decide. This book presents solutions. At the same time, it will take monumental courage to engage them.

CAN WE SAVE THE REST OF THE WORLD FROM HUMAN OVERPOPULATION?

While first world countries maintain replacement level birth rates of two children per woman or less, the developing world countries scream ahead with 83,000,000 new babies, net gain, annually.(10)

Unfortunately, ancient religions such as the Catholic Church, Islam, Hindu and other faiths press their followers toward accelerating birth rates. Thus, the United Nations projects that humans remain on course by adding 1.0 billion added, net gain, every 12 years and more than likely will exceed 2.2 billion more humans to reach in excess of 10 billion by 2050. Some demographers tabulate that humans will hit 14 billion before the end of the century, or more!

So, the question remains? Can first world countries save the rest of the world by allowing endless immigration?

Blatant and sobering answer: **not a chance!**

If you look at the Roy Beck five-minute video, **"Immigration, Gumballs and Poverty,"** by downloading it at www.numbersusa.org, you will see that no first world nation can receive that accelerating line of desperate migrants if those countries hope to survive the 21st century. Their sheer numbers are too overwhelming.

What's the answer? Help them in their own countries with water extraction, teach them how to grow crops and ultimately, but most importantly, help them with access to birth control.

If that doesn't work, unfortunately, Mother Nature will respond with her own answers. As noted earlier, she operates like the Terminator: no mercy, no guilt, no concern, no empathy, and nothing but death as her solution.

As human population gallops toward 10 billion, those starvation deaths must accelerate as arable land and water diminish under humanity's onslaught.

Worldwide, about 1.5 to 1.9 billion people cannot obtain clean drinking water. In India, the Indian Express Newspaper reported that 60.4 percent of Indians cannot access a toilet. Thus, they do their business on the land and into the rivers. The Ganges remains an open sewer conveyor belt transporting trillions of gallons of contaminated water into the Indian Ocean 24/7. As reported by Bill Ryerson, project director of Population Media, 2,195 Indian children die 24/7 from diarrhea, dysentery and other water borne diseases. Yet, India grows by 14 million, net gain, annually. (Source: www.populationmedia.org)

The same degradation of humanity occurs in Africa where the majority of people use the land as a toilet. Their fecal matter dries until it wafts into lakes and rivers. No one can drink from open water sources.

WHAT WILL THE FUTURE LOOK LIKE IF WE CONTINUE ON COURSE TO ADD ANOTHER 100, 200, 300 MILLION MORE PEOPLE INTO THE UNITED STATES?

As a world bicycle traveler, I crossed six continents to see overpopulation dilemmas across the globe at a snail's pace of 12 miles per hour. When you travel that slowly, you see the vacant eyes and hopelessness of starving people one-by-one. You witness gaunt bodies. You stare at the tragedy of their movements. You see illiteracy, diseases, contaminated water, filthy conditions, grinding poverty and another dozen miseries for billions of people.

Once a country grows itself into overpopulation, its citizens exist rather than live. Once the numbers manifest, every person subsists in a sort of mental, emotional and spiritual purgatory. They can't escape. And, they can't do anything about their plight. Yes, a few make it to Canada, Australia, America and Europe. But 99 percent of humanity can't and won't make it out of their countries. They must live in the country of their birth.

As you will see in this book, if the United States continues on its present population growth path, it will disintegrate or devolve into a third world country. It may not happen in 10 years, and/or maybe 20 years—but as you read the research in this book, at some point, our country cannot help but sink into unsolvable water shortages, energy exhaustion, resource depletion and scant arable land.

And the one item everyone avoids or denies: oil will be exhausted within this century, per Christopher Clugston's book **Blip**, probably by 2050. Once that occurs, every citizen of every color, religion and class will be adversely affected as to starvation and total collapse of our oil-driven industrial civilization. These quotes forecast America's future:

"The cheap oil age created an artificial bubble of plentitude for a period not much longer than a human lifetime....so I hazard to assert that as oil ceases to be cheap and the world reserves move toward depletion, we will be left with an enormous population...that the ecology of the earth will not support. The journey back toward non-oil population homeostasis will not be pretty. We will discover the hard way that population hyper growth was simply a side-effect of the oil age. It was a condition, not a problem with a solution. That is what happened, and we are stuck with it." James Howard Kunstler, The Long Emergency

"Oil depletion and climate change will create and entirely new context which political struggles will be played out. Within that context, it is not just about freedom, democracy and equality that are at stake, but the survival of billions of humans and of entire ecosystems." Richard Heinberg, Peak Everything

"There is a major problem of unsustainability of our environment, and we're seeing it in our natural resources, peak oil is probably upon us, and it can't be sustained. We're on an unsustainable path, and at this point in history, we are responsible for that. We are going to have to change our ways." Michael Ruppert

"We're at peak oil, peak water, peak resources, and so either we figure it out and let science lead or we head down a very bad, dark trail to where a lot of people aren't going to make it." Henry Rollins

SECTION I

THE DEADLIEST BIRTH RATE
AFFECTING ALL HUMANITY

CHAPTER I

///

FIRST DEADLIEST BIRTHRATE AFFECTING ALL HUMANITY: AFRICA

"I am convinced that some political and social activities and practices of the Catholic organizations are detrimental and even dangerous for the community as a whole, here, and everywhere. I mention here in America only the fight against birth control at a time when overpopulation in various countries has become a serious threat to the health of the people and a grave obstacle to any attempt to organize peace on this planet." Albert Einstein

Africa's exploding birthrates, water shortages, food scarcity, and animal extinctions portend a harsh future for humans and animals alike.

As immigration, both legal and illegal, continues flooding into the United States of America—refugees also pour into Canada, Australia and Europe. Note that all Western countries stabilized their populations via birth control since 1970 by averaging 2.0 children or less per female.

Unfortunately, as first world countries created stable and sustainable societies since 1970, their leaders chose unending immigration from overloaded developing countries. For example, in the United States, the late Senator Teddy Kennedy, Jacob Javits and Howard Metzenbaum created the 1965 Immigration Reform Act (Hart-Celler Act of the 89th Congress and signed by Lyndon Baines Johnson) that jumped America's population from 200 million to 300 million people by October of 2006.

If continued, that same act expects to add another 139 million people within 29 years by 2050. Note: we're already 30 million into that number at 330 million in 2021 on our way to 439 million. Much the same immigrant ingress occurs in Canada, Europe and Australia. Where do those immigrants originate? Answer: the developing countries that add 83 million people, net gain, annually.

Unknown to most countries and people living on this planet, an accelerating birthrate in Africa threatens all Western civilizations in the 21st century. At 1.3 billion in 2021, Africa accelerates toward 2.0 billion by 2050 and 4.0 billion by the end of this century. (Source: "Africa's Population Projections" by United Nations 2016)

As an example, the average Burundian woman births 6.3 children, double the international fertility rate. Burundians expect to jump from 10 million to 20 million in two decades. Egypt, currently 98 million, expects to reach 160 million by 2050. Ethiopia, at 98 million, expects to double to 210 million by 2060. (Source: UN "Africa's Population Projections"; Egypt Independent, July 5, 2019, "Egypt's population to increase 60 million by 2050.")

Ironically, Egypt imports most of its food to feed its current population in 2021. As the human race adds 1.0 billion more people, net gain, every 12 years, Africa expects to quadruple its population within 79 years. Africans grow so fast; they cannot water, feed, house, educate or sustain the expected 4.0 billion people about to appear on that continent.

What does it mean? It means that every living creature featuring feathers, hooves, claws, fins or fur that lives in Africa will become food for the human mob. It means relentless extinction of rhinos, lions, gazelles, wildebeest, giraffes and elephants—just about any creature that breathes.

Nonetheless, the Pope condemns birth control in Africa. Islam promotes as many children as possible as it expands across the globe by birthrates and/or jihad. World leaders see the carnage, poverty, disease and futility of Africa in 2021, but fail to call for a world conference to discuss what's coming and what can be done to change course.

Therefore, those burgeoning populations flood into first world countries with no end to the line.

Question: what will humans do once the planet reaches another added 2.2 billion people by 2050—a scant 29 years from now? Won't they need to be watered, fed, housed, warmed and sustained in a finite world with finite resources? If you think the flood of another 1.0 million refugees knocking on Europe's door today spells disaster for the civilized West, what do you think any Western country faces in the next 79 years when Africa hits 4.0 billion desperate people? When does it cease to be the West's responsibility to care for this endless stream of humanity?

According to www.cis.org with research by Dr. Steven Camarota, the illegal alien flow jumped back to 500,000 illegal alien border crossers in 2014-2015. In other words, the line never ends as Mexico, at 129 million in 2021, remains on course to add another 16 million people to reach 145 million by mid-century. (Source: www.populationpyramid.net)

Canada, Europe and Australia follow suit with their own immigrant numbers measuring into the hundreds of thousands, and ultimately, millions.

One look at Minneapolis, Minnesota shows 120,000 African Somalian legal refugees now overwhelming welfare services across that city. Yet, Somalia at 16 million in 2021, expects to reach 33 million by 2050. In other words, double its already overpopulated country! Is there any chance that America or Canada can solve Somalia's birthrates by absorbing an endless line of millions of refugees?

"Somalia is rapidly expanding with almost three percent annual population growth and a high fertility rate of 6.26 children per woman, which is the 4th highest in the world." (Source: United Nations "Population Projections.")

Similar scenarios occur in Sweden, Norway, Belgium, Denmark, France, Germany and Italy as to immigrants' onslaught.

Question to ask yourself and your kids: what is the point of endless immigration from Somalia in 2021 when that country, along with the rest of Africa, refuses or can't solve its own birth rates? What's the point of adding more of their people to Western countries to become like the countries they fled?

How do you think your kids will survive the onslaught? What are you doing to raise a national-international discussion on human overpopulation? What kind of a civilization do you expect to bequeath to your children? Answer: if Western countries continue on the same path, every nation will become overpopulated where everyone suffers, and no one may lead anything like "quality of life" or a decent standard of living. Not to mention a degrading environment!

Einstein said, "The problems in the world today are so enormous, they cannot be solved with the level of thinking that created them."

None of us will escape the growing consequences of Africa's population bomb.

CHAPTER 2

///

SECOND DEADLIEST BIRTHRATE AFFECTING ALL HUMANITY: INDIA

"Overpopulation will destroy it all. I use what I call my bathroom metaphor. If two people live in an apartment, and there are two bathrooms, then both have freedom of the bathroom. Each may go to the bathroom any time, and stay as long as they want for whatever their need. And everyone believes in the freedom of the bathroom. But if you have 20 people in the apartment and two bathrooms, no matter how much every person believes in freedom of the bathroom, there is no such thing. You have to set up times for each person, you have to bang at the door, "Aren't you through yet?" And in the same way, democracy cannot survive overpopulation. Human dignity cannot survive it. Convenience and decency cannot survive it. As you put more and more people onto the world, the value of life not only declines, but it disappears." Isaac Asimov, writer

In 1960, India reached 500,000,000 people. Today, driven by multiple ancient religions that prohibit birth control, India suffers every kind of social, infrastructure and environmental consequence known to humanity with its 1.3 billion people. Even more catastrophic, it adds 14 million more people, net gain, annually on its way to 1.6 billion by 2050.

India's major river, the Ganges, which I once rafted, flows into the Indian Ocean with the most polluted, toxic and contaminated waters known to humankind—along with and endless flotilla of plastic. It features trillions of gallons of untreated sewage, industrial waste, hundreds of chemicals and millions of pieces of plastics—that flow into the Indian

Ocean 24/7. That watery, chemicalized conveyer belt creates a 20,000 square mile dead zone at the mouth of the Ganges. Indians think it's a sacred river, but there's nothing sacred about it. Once it hits the Indian Ocean, those contaminated waters spread all over the planet—poisoning marine life, avian life, reefs, the ocean floor and cause deadly acidification around the globe.

Of note, Africa, China, Indonesia, Sri Lanka, Philippines and India dump the most plastics into the world's oceans. Latest estimates show 5.25 trillion pieces of plastic float above and flow under the surface around the world—killing millions of marine creatures annually. (11)

According to Isabelle Autissier, President of World Wildlife Fund France: "More than 310 million tons of plastic waste were generated in 2016, one third of which ended up in Nature. The report is damning and has dramatic consequences for the environment, human health and the economy. The impact on biodiversity is particularly striking: to date, animals from more than 270 species have been entangled and more than 240 have ingested plastic."

As per investigations by marine biologist Julia Whitty, published in **Onearth Magazine**, 46,000 pieces of plastic trash float on every square mile of Earth's oceans. In a word: sickening! Why? Because we've known this for 20 years, but no action to stop it has occurred by creating incentive-driven deposit-return laws internationally. Plastics make an effective "extinction machine." (Source: www.unesco.org, The United Nations Environmental Program estimated in 2006 that every square mile of ocean contains 46,000 pieces of floating plastic. Once discarded, plastics are weathered and eroded into very small fragments known as micro-plastics.)

Whitty said, "When we hear of extinction, most of us think of the plight of the rhino, tiger, panda, or blue whale. The overall numbers are terrifying. Of the 40,168 species that the 10,000 scientists in the World Conservation Union have assessed, 1 in 4 mammals, 1 in 8 birds, 1 in 3 amphibians, 1 in 3 conifers are at risk of extinction. The peril faced by other classes of organisms is less thoroughly analyzed, but fully 40 percent of the examined species of planet Earth are in danger, including up to 51 percent of reptiles, 52 percent of insects, and 73 percent of flowering plants."

As a personal note, nothing compares to the abject immorality of humanity more than destruction and extinction of other life forms on this planet by our hands.

To repeat what I reported earlier, every day of the year, 2,195 Indian children under the age of 12, die of dysentery, diarrhea and other waterborne diseases die from drinking contaminated water. (12) (Source: www.populationmedia.org, www.ncbi.nim.nih.gov)

Yet, as India's population accelerates by 14 to 16 million net gain annually, they grow so fast, they cannot solve any of their problems. Disease and squalor top the "human misery index" beyond the comprehension of citizens from Western countries.

India cannot support jobs, classrooms and housing for that many people added annually. Yet, not one word about population stabilization comes from India's leaders. At one point, Indira Gandhi attempted to bring birth control to India when I visited in 1984, but she failed because of religious-cultural norms that overpowered reasoned thinking. By 2050, India will become the most populated country on the planet at 1.6 billion people according to U.N. projections.

If you look at the beauty of the Taj Mahal, one of the most famous landmarks of India, a short trip to the river next to it shows millions of pieces of plastic clogging its waters. And, the water features endless chemical poisons leaving it unfit for human or animal use. Thus, extraordinary architectural achievement on the one hand, but ugly, destructive and horrific human folly next to it. What kind of cultures tolerate such dichotomies? In Indian cities like Mumbai, air pollution poisons the lungs of everyone breathing that toxic air 24/7. You see citizens tapping into electrical wires illegally at every juncture. You see filth, trash, and garbage everywhere. You cannot imagine the smell of stench! Indians toss their trash endlessly. It's not within their culture to pick up rubbish. When you see the traffic, it's a free-for-all that confounds and confuses the Western mind. The National Nutritional Monitoring Bureau estimates that only 15 percent of Indians receive adequate nourishment daily.

On top of those conditions, no elected officials move to improve India's sanitation infrastructure, education systems or birth control. They grind along, decade after decade, in horrible poverty, illiteracy and misery.

As can be imagined, because of adding that 14 million more people annually, India's wilderness suffers encroachment via roads, housing, mining, lumbering and other development. Animal extinction rates soar in India. The Bengal Tiger and the Snow Leopard will not survive in the wilds within several decades. Elephants face an uncertain future. Birds of all kinds face extinction from loss of habitat. Fish and plants vanish as Indians invade and demolish habitat.

Whitty said, "By the most conservative measure—the current rate of extinction is 100 times the background rate. But eminent Harvard biologist Edward O. Wilson estimates that the true rate is more like 1,000 to 10,000 times the background rate. The actual annual sum is only an educated guess, because no scientist believes the tally of life ends at the 1.5 million species already discovered. Bracketed between best-and-worst-case scenarios, then, somewhere between 2.7 and 270 species are erased from existence every day."

Can you imagine that humanity has increased the extinction rate in the last century some 100 to 1,000 times that of the background extinction rate? How can that be moral, ethical or rational?

With all the realities facing the people of India, no one raises a finger to address their population predicament. Even in the face of so much human misery, their leaders live in "cognitive dissonance" also known as "intellectual denial of reality." You almost question if they possess any degree of higher intelligence to make reasonable choices, but then, you realize that America, Canada, Australia and Europe follow the same path. (We'll talk about leadership stupidity in a later chapter.)

Whitty continued, "We now understand that the majority of life on Earth has never been—and will never be—known to us."

Edward O. Wilson predicts that our present course will lead to the extinction of half of all plant and animal species by the year 2100. He also stated that we will probably eradicate a full third of animal and plant life by 2050. (Source: May 2007, Mother Jones News, "Gone: Mass Extinction and the Hazards of Earth's Vanishing Biodiversity.")

Please realize that this book covers only the tip of the iceberg. At any time, we may witness horrific outbreaks of cholera and other diseases that will kill millions of humans in Asia. Covid, in 2020 and 2021, already rages across that continent.

But what does it mean for all of us in the USA or other western countries like Canada, Europe and Australia?

To be blunt, we face a global mess that will ultimately arrive on a big platter and shoved down our throats. Today, millions of Indians clamor for visas to move to the USA, Europe, Australia and Canada. The rich ones buy their way into America. Some Indians discovered how to gain U.S. government loans to buy all the motels across America. They continue accelerated chain-migration with that motel-niche. Whatever it takes to flee the hell-hole of India, they're taking it.

As with 50,000 annual Diversity Visas, 14 million people apply annually to gain the "Golden Ticket" to America.

If you think the refugee crisis facing Europe the last two years was bad and continuing in 2021—you haven't seen anything yet.

When India starts facing hunger crises via lack of arable land, dwindling rainfall, and growing 'catastrophic climate destabilization' with its 1.3 billion people—we're all in trouble. **In 2021, we watch a global disaster in the making.**

No amount of immigration solves anything for Indians. No amount of international aid will help them. Why? Because they keep growing their human numbers beyond any solutions.

As you read this book, yes, pretty sobering! In fact, pretty distressing! **Because if you're in your 30's or 40's, you and your children will see this international debacle on a stage unseen in human history.** That's why America, Australia, Europe and Canada must create an international discussion-debate on human population stabilization—before Mother Nature does it for us.

Eleanor Roosevelt said it 50 years ago: *"We must prevent human tragedy rather than run around trying to save ourselves after an event has already occurred. Unfortunately, history clearly shows that we arrive at catastrophe by failing to meet the situation, by failing to act when we should have acted. The opportunity passes us by, and the next disaster is always more difficult and compounded than the last one."*

That's why for the past 20 years, I have pitched directors and producers to interview on "60 Minutes"; National Public Radio; Public Broadcasting Service, and the New York Times along with dozens of top newspapers. Unfortunately, they've ignored my queries annually.

Or, if you live in Canada, Europe and Australia, work to promote your own leaders to top spots on television to expose what we all face. In Canada, Madeline Weld, Dan Murray and Tim Murray. In Australia, Mark O'Connor, Jenny Goldie and Dick Smith. In the United Kingdom, Brian McGavin, Eric Rimmer and others.

CHAPTER 3

///

THIRD DEADLIEST BIRTHRATE AFFECTING ALL HUMANITY: CHINA

"Overpopulation is the biggest problem facing us, and immigration is a part of that problem. It has to be addressed." David Brower, Sierra Club

As a naïve, youthful world bicycle traveler back in 1984, I toured through China when it opened to international visitors. You can imagine my joy—fulfilling my teenage dream to walk on the "Great Wall of China."

But what really impacted me: wall-to-wall people. Every piece of land bloomed with crops. Every nook and cranny filled with people! They jammed every city. They overflowed every sector of that ancient land. Their plight stunned me. Today, they drive down 50 lane freeways and breathe toxic air along with horrifically polluted rivers like the Yangtze. That one visit changed my life by changing my perceptions concerning the end result of too many people.

At the time, Dr. Paul Ehrlich's, **The Population Bomb,** described the horrific consequences of overpopulation. However, the mainstream media degraded him and his figures. Today, his figures play-out on a world scale even more terrifying than when he wrote the book: 4.0 million children die of starvation annually. Another 9.0 million adults die from lack of food, annually. (13) (14) (Source: United Nations)

Another 1.5 to 2.0 billion cannot secure clean drinking water. Billions live in what social scientists call "The Human Misery Index". Hopeless, helpless and no way to change it! (15) (Source: www.WorldHealthOrganization.org)

Unfortunately, all of Ehrlich's detractors never visited India or China. Their worldviews stemmed from their limited experiences in America, Canada or Europe. They echoed the notorious economist Julian Simon's boasts that this planet housed enough resources for 10,000 years for unlimited numbers of humans. Dr. Albert Bartlett, University of Colorado, named him an "innumerate" or *mathematically illiterate.*

Later, economist Kenneth Boulding, University of Colorado, stated, "Anyone who thinks we can continue population expansion is either an economist or a madman."

All the while, humans add another 83 million, net gain, of themselves to this planet, annually. Even with one child per woman birthrates in China for 42 years, because of "population momentum" (so many women birthing one child), China adds 8.0 million annually, net gain. They expect to add 100 million by 2050 to reach 1.5 billion. (16) (Source: www. macrotrends.net)

While China continues its human numbers explosion, it degrades its quality of life and standard of living to levels beyond our understanding. Countless Chinese families live in high-rise box apartments of 200 square feet or less. China charges toward endless concrete jungles for its cities, vanishing wilderness that creates severe animal extinction rates and a complete breakdown of ecology as to air, water and soil.

China constructs one new coal-fired electrical plant every week of the year. It adds 27,000,000 (million) new cars, net gain, annually according to an NBC Nightly News report with Lester Holt. It suffers under toxic air pollution so severe that lung cancer rates explode in big cities like Shanghai and Beijing. You cannot believe it until you see it; I visited those cities to see it up close and ugly.

While the world burns 99 million barrels of oil 24/7 in 2021, experts predict that China expects to burn 98 million barrels of oil annually by 2030—a scant nine years from now. (Source: **The Long Emergency** by James Howard Kunstler)

While everyone wants to drop the 'carbon footprint' from fossil fuel exhaust, all the efforts of www.350.org equate to futility. Meanwhile, all of humanity faces "catastrophic climate destabilization" such as what happened in New Orleans, Baton Rouge, Mexico Beach, Houston and many other cities along the Gulf Coast. Additionally, Sandy on the East Coast and the Haiyan typhoon in the Philippines!

In 2017, I bicycled coast-to-coast across the northern tier of America. I pedaled through a 240,000-acre fire in Montana east of Great Falls. My cycling mates and I inhaled smoke for an entire day and witnessed a blackened landscape for 360 degrees for over 50 miles. In 2018, my wife Sandi and I pedaled down the West Coast to witness Washington, Oregon and California burning up with multiple, massive wildfires. In 2020, Washington State, Oregon, California, Montana and Colorado watched millions of acres burned to a crisp. It's only going to worsen as we destabilize Earth's biosphere with our carbon emissions. Again, the cause: exceptional drought conditions.

On the world scale, all that carbon exhaust suffocates the oceans as they "ingest" that exhaust-waste dumped into our biosphere. Results vary from "acidified" oceans that kill reefs because normal "pH" balance no longer exists. Thus, phyto-planktons that create 80 percent of our oxygen supply appear to be in grave danger. Worldwide reefs die out at an ever-increasing rate of speed.

China's water usage, energy usage, food consumption and resource depletion reach unimaginable stratospheric levels as they mechanize everything in order to grow into the wealth of Western countries. But before the middle of this century, China, along with all fossil-fuel-driven civilizations, must contend with the end of oil: (to repeat this quote)

"The cheap oil age created an artificial bubble of plentitude for a period not much longer than a human lifetime....so I hazard to assert that as oil ceases to be cheap and the world reserves move toward depletion, we will be left with an enormous population...that the ecology of the earth will not support. The journey back toward non-oil population homeostasis will not be pretty. We will discover the hard way that population hyper growth was simply a side-effect of the oil age. It was a condition, not a problem with a solution. That is what happened, and we are stuck with it." James Howard Kunstler, The Long Emergency

If the energy crisis doesn't impact China, water shortages most certainly will.

By 2020 The Water Issue to Affect 30 to 40 Percent of the World

"It's a huge problem that the electrical sector does not realize how much water they actually consume. And together with the fact that we do not have unlimited water resources, it could lead to a serious crisis if nobody acts on it soon," said Professor Benjamin, Sovacool from Aarhus University.

When you include the agricultural sector with vanishing ground water, a "Perfect Demographic Storm" builds throughout China and India as well as Bangladesh.

As to China's rivers, the Yangtze River dumps trillions of gallons of lethal waste into the oceans 24/7. It features an astounding 20,000 square mile "dead zone" at its mouth. That means all vertebrate marine creatures cannot live within those toxic waters. Dozens of such poisoned rivers flow into the ocean from China. Nonetheless, those toxic waters flow around the world to poison marine habitats everywhere. (17) (Source: www.cs.mun.ca)

You cannot comprehend China's ordeal unless you visited that ancient civilization. **China is out of control of itself**. I'm only touching the surface of China's predicament. As it continues adding eight million people, net gain, annually, every problem it faces only worsens by a factor of 8,000,000—to the point of "NO" solutions and total breakdown.

But the Chinese show exceptional intelligence in escaping to first world countries. Today, Chinese immigrants commandeer Vancouver, British Columbia in Canada as they've grown to a 65 percent dominance of the once 100 percent Canadian population. They buy land and buildings. Chinese dictate to the Canadians as they dominate schools and local governments. They chain-migrate their families into Canada.

As this enormous flood of humanity adds 1.0 billion every 12 years and a total of 2.2 billion added by mid-century to rise from 7.8 billion in 2021 to 10 billion in 2050—everyone and all of us, and every Western nation faces horrific environmental consequences, quality of life degradation and immigration consequences on a scale unknown in all of our history as a species.

Share these videos all over America:

In a five minute astoundingly simple yet brilliant video, **"Immigration, Poverty, and Gum Balls"**, Roy Beck, director of www. numbersusa.ORG, graphically illustrates the impact of overpopulation. Take five minutes to see for yourself:

http://www.youtube.com/watch?v=LPjzfGChGlE&feature=player embedded

"Immigration by the numbers—off the chart" by Roy Beck

This 10-minute demonstration shows Americans the results of unending mass immigration on the quality of life and sustainability for future generations: in a few words, "Mind boggling!" www. NumbersUSA.org

http://www.youtube.com/watch?v=muw22wTePqQ

You will find more options for action in the last three chapters.

CHAPTER 4

///

RECIPIENT NATIONS OF BIRTHRATE OVERLOAD: AMERICA, CANADA, EUROPE, AUSTRALIA

"The wealthy nations and wealthy consumers have the greatest impact, but sheer numbers do count. There are ways that we can stabilize the human population without unpleasantly imposed restrictions, namely with universal women's rights, education and available contraception."
Rex Weyler, Greenpeace Co-Founder

How did the first three chapters affect you? Did you understand the enormity of what humanity faces in the next 29 years? How about the rest of the plant and animal life on this planet? What about the oceans? What about quality of life? What about your children?

Are you astounded that the mainstream media suppresses this demographic issue at all costs? Why? Answer: they lack intellectual comprehension that they will not escape its grip on them or their children. Catholics via the Pope, Islam, Hindus, Christians and virtually all religions stand in denial of this demographic juggernaut bearing down on humanity.

Yes, the media reports every consequence of overpopulation as to worldwide hunger, water shortages, species extinctions, wars for resources and catastrophic climate destabilization. But no one, not one world leader addresses or attempts to speak up on what we face.

As you can see, no one will escape the ramifications of the next added 3.0 billion people to this globe. No one will escape the implications of adding 100 million more people to America within 29 years. You may expect those population consequences to invade your state, your community and your family.

Remember this: developing country citizens will not stop their birth rates significantly enough to stop overloading their countries.

In 2021, the United Nations estimates that 60 million refugees lack water, food, energy and homes, and look toward first world countries to migrate. Their numbers will grow to 150 million to as high as 200,000 million by 2050.

What Western Countries Face with Refugee Armada

Canada houses 38,000,000 people in 2021. Because of mass immigration, they expect 44,000,000 by 2050. It could very well be another 10 million on top of that if Justin Trudeau, their Prime Minister gets his way to dramatically increase the immigrant flow. To give you an idea of Canada's dilemma, let's look at the numbers. We know Canada as a "big" little country. That means it's "big" in landmass but lacks ample arable land to grow crops. While its citizens chose 2.0 birth rates since 1970, its leaders forced massive immigration onto Canada. It faces food shortages, environmental breakdown, accelerating carbon footprint damage, species extinctions and lowered quality of life.

Europe houses 742.5 million people in 2021. It encompasses 3.9 million square miles. Not much bigger than the United States at 3.1 million square miles. The United Kingdom houses 67 million people in a landmass less than the size of Oregon. Oregon features 4.0 million people. Germany at 82 million holds less land than the State of New Mexico. That state holds 1.8 million. The tiny country of France holds 66 million. While Europe faces tremendous overcrowding today, it faces mass immigration overrunning every border of all of its countries from Middle Eastern and African population overload.

Australia holds 24 million in 2021, but expects to reach 38 to 48 million by mid-century via mass immigration. It lacks water and arable land, but powerful developer interests force immigration onto that desert continent as if tomorrow will never arrive. Note: over 90 percent of Australia features desert. How do I know? I cycled around the entire perimeter of that continent in 1984 to 1985. I encountered hellish heat, endless desert, bush flies, camels, kangaroos, wombats, frilled lizards, boab trees, termite mounds and bush fires. What was I thinking?

In contrast, the USA holds 330 million in a landmass at 3.1 million square miles, but as you saw from the immigration invasion, America expects 439 million by 2050 and 625 million at the end of this century.

Can enough activists be inspired from a book like this to create a movement to stop mass immigration into Western countries? Goal: we need a national discussion-debate on the future of our civilization. It's not going to happen by itself. That discussion-debate begins with you.

SECTION 2

WHAT OUR CIVILIZATION FACES: IT'S THE LITTLE THINGS THAT ADD UP TO BIG PROBLEMS

CHAPTER 5

///

ACCELERATING POPULATION GROWTH CONSEQUENCES

"I believe climate change is the defining environmental issue of our time. It's hurting our people — around the world — and it's time to stand up and say we've had enough. Enough of rising seas and widening deserts that threaten our homes and our crops. Enough of withering drought and blistering heat that mean more malnutrition and disease. Enough of raging floods, wildfires and storms that threaten people everywhere with one disaster after another." Robert Redford, actor

What did Redford mean by that rather abrupt statement?

Here's another harsh reality: United Nations population projections show Bangladesh to grow from 161 million to 201 million by 2050. Is that totally insane or what? (18) (Source: www.populationpyramid.net)

In an earlier quote, Dr. Henry Kendall talked about halting population growth with "compassion and justice." What does that mean? Answer: it means humans need to take their fecundity rates into their own hands and provide for birth control that brings human populations into balance with the carrying capacity of the planet.

Exponential growth cannot and will not be tolerated by Mother Nature. She already starves to death over 4.0 million children annually and another 9.0 million adults. That's the "...will be done by nature, brutally and without pity..." aspect of Dr. Kendall's statement.

Redford points out the changes in our climate that will bring about horrendous consequences to all species living on this planet.

What constitutes exponential growth? The term means: endless growth of any organism. That growth ultimately results in overwhelming the carrying capacity of area in which it thrives and finally, collapse and ultimately extinction of that species.

As it stands today, according to the United Kingdom Oxford University's the late Norman Myers, human encroachment upon worldwide habitat causes the extinction of 100 species daily. (Note that E.O. Wilson's report shows up to 270 species daily vanish from the planet. Chapter 4.) That means those creatures no longer exist because humanity overwhelms its own carrying capacity and destroys the food, water and living area for other species. Thus, humanity creates the most dangerous aspect of Mother Nature's "carrying capacity" limits. The current rate of extinctions for plants and animals within the United States runs the dozens annually. (Source: U.S. Department of Interior)

"The current rate of extinction is up to 10,000 times higher than the average historical extinction rates. We humans are almost wholly responsible for this increase. We don't know exactly how many species go extinct every year, but it could be 100,000-about 1 every 5 minutes." (Source: www.theworldcounts.com/.../species-extinction-rate.)

Collapsed civilizations litter our history books: Easter Island, Mayan Empire, Incas, Anasazi, Vikings, Rwanda, Haiti and more to come. Read Jared Diamond's: **Collapse—How societies choose to fail or succeed.**

Those civilizations collapsed via exhaustion of food or water, i.e., they overwhelmed their carrying capacity.

Today, nearly all of humanity overrides its carrying capacity in oil-driven and oil-fed countries. Without oil, the United States could not exist with its 330 million inhabitants. Without the diesel-filled tractors planting and harvesting enormous amounts of food, we could not feed the current number of people in the USA.

The late geologist Walter Youngquist said, **"This is going to be an interesting decade, for the perfect storm is brewing—energy, immigration and oil imports. China grows in direct confrontation for remaining oil. I think the USA is on a big, slippery downhill slope. Will the thin veneer of civilization survive?"**

Youngquist continued, "Beyond oil, population is the number one problem of the 21st century, for when oil is gone as we know and use it today—and it WILL be gone—population will still be here."

He states the obvious. Unfortunately, by 2050, humans will have used up most of the oil on the planet. Our current rate of 99 million barrels per day pales in comparison of the predicted usage by China by 2030 of 98 million barrels daily. With the added 2.2 billion humans, oil usage will grow to over 200 million barrels burned daily. The carbon footprint havoc on our biosphere and oceans will prove cataclysmic. (Source: **The Long Emergency** by James Howard Kunstler)

When you look back on history's ragged mane, those collapsed civilizations passed into oblivion without much fanfare. But with major cities like Los Angeles sporting 11 million; New York City with 8.3 million; Mexico City with 19 million; Bombay with 20 million; Sao Paulo with 20 million; Delhi with 28 million; Tokyo featuring 37 million; Shanghai at 28 million, and all the other overloaded cities around the world—it becomes obvious that humanity cannot exist without oil—but oil will soon vanish. Unfortunately, nothing on technology's horizon can duplicate the energy we receive from oil. To say it's going to get ugly with that many people bunched up in those cities may be the understatement of the 21st century.

At the end of Kendall's statement, he said, "…and will leave a ravaged world." You may appreciate the "Seven wonders of the world" created by human beings. Glorious triumphs of architecture and human engineering! However, we could add the **"Seven tragedies of the world"** created by humans such as the Great Pacific Garbage Patch, Sixth Extinction Session, Overly Polluted Biosphere, Acidified and Contaminated Oceans, Acid Rain Phenomenon, Destruction of Worldwide Rainforests, Human Misery Index and more to come.

We may prove ourselves a clever species, but none too smart. None too reasoning. None too rational. None too proactive.

Can America lead the world in this quest for a sustainable future?

We need to get busy in order to provide a livable world for all creatures including ourselves.

CHAPTER 6

//

ENDLESS ADDITIONS CREATE ENDLESS SHORTAGES

"Most Western elites continue urging the wealthy West not to stem the migrant tide [that adds 80 million net gain annually to the planet], but to absorb our global brothers and sisters until their horrid ordeal has been endured and shared by all—ten billion humans packed onto an ecologically devastated planet." Otis Graham, Unguarded Gates

When Graham wrote his book, he uncovered uncomfortable aspects of humanity's race toward endless population growth on a finite planet. Let's examine what he addressed that you see summed up in the quote above.

To repeat from the Introduction of this book, each year, with the current world population of 7.8 billion human beings, an average of 60 million people die from all causes—old age, war, disease, starvation and other violence. Not only does human fecundity replace that 60 million people who died, it adds another 83 million to total 143 million newborn babies every year of every decade without pause. Demographic projections indicate the human race could very well reach 14 billion by the end of the century.

(Source: www.medindia.net/patients/calculators/world-death-clock.asp)

First of all, with that huge number of newborn offspring, the countries that give births to that many people cannot educate them. Thus, illiteracy, the barometer for all poverty and human misery—accelerates. Further, they cannot feed them.

As you can imagine, misery dominates. The eruptions in Africa in the past several years revolved around food crises. Egypt alone with its 98.5 million subsisting on desert sands expects to reach 160 million by mid-century. Egypt depends on grains from the West to feed its human multitude, yet as oil depletes and costs more, Egyptians will not be able to buy food. They face mass starvation. Hundreds of thousands live on the brink in Somalia, Sudan, Congo, Kenya and South Africa. All of Asia lives on the edge. A full 1.5 to 2.0 billion human beings worldwide cannot secure a clean glass of water daily. You will see repetition of these figures at several points in the book to really "impact" you with the enormity of what humanity faces.

Nonetheless, political leaders of the world, religious leaders of the world and the developing countries of the world refuse to take action. The human mob accelerates without a word from NBC's Lester Holt, ABC's David Muir or CBS' Norah O'Donnell. The same applies to NPR's Robert Seigel, Terry Gross, Steve Inskeep and others. It also applies to PBS, CNN and FOX. Three years ago, ABC's David Muir raced around Somalia when 100,000 children faced immediate starvation—but that crisis quickly lost the public eye and the children continued starving.

How Many Refugees Are in the World?

According to www.brycs.org, a 2009 report by the United Nations refugee agency (UNHCR), 42 million people around the world were uprooted from their homes due to conflict or persecution. Of this number, 16 million were considered refugees, while 26 million were displaced within their own countries or were considered asylum-seekers in other countries. Approximately 45 percent of the world's refugees are under 18-years-old. About 80 percent of the world's refugees are hosted by developing countries. The largest refugee producing countries at present include Afghanistan, Iraq, Somali and Sudan, while Colombia, Iraq, Sudan and the Democratic Republic of the Congo have the largest internally displaced populations. At present, Venezuela in South America suffers horrific food scarcity.

Please note this population projection: At present, South America carries 432.9 million people. They are projected to rise to 779 million within 29 years. Why would anyone choose that nightmare of a future? (Source: South America Population Projections, www.cepal.org)

Some estimates by the UN show in excess of 60 million refugees looking for a new country to move to by 2050. A recent survey found:

More Than 100 Million Worldwide Dream of a Life in the U.S.

More than 25 percent in Liberia, Sierra Leone, Dominican Republic want to move to the U.S. See:

http://www.gallup.com/poll/161435/100-million-worldwide-dream-life.aspx

However, no one ever asks the most logical question: when will the immigrant line to first world countries end? Answer: the line grows by 83 million net gain annually, which means the line never ends, but grows and expands and grows.

On the outskirts of hundreds of modern cities in Asia, you see millions living in slums. Millions trashing the waterways with their garbage and human waste. Yet, no one takes action to stop this proliferation of human population explosion. In fact, the Pope and Islamic churches encourage more births no matter how much human misery.

Since developing countries refuse to engage birth control for cultural and religious reasons, they use first world countries for a human exhaust valve. But, at some point, countries like the United States, Canada, Europe and Australia will exceed their carrying capacity—resulting in water shortages, food crises, energy depletion and resource exhaustion.

Africa, India, Indonesia, Mexico, the Middle East and Bangladesh continue growing their populations without pause.

As soon as their refugees flood into first world countries, those refugees grow their carbon footprint impact, water footprint, energy footprint and ecological footprint 10 to 100 times greater than they impacted the environment in their native countries.

I remember my travels through Hong Kong where thousands and thousands of people live in 100 square foot "coffin" apartments. You cannot imagine the human degradation of spirit from lack of connection to the Natural World, when you live in a 100 square foot apartment. I know because I stayed in them when I visited. We must ask ourselves how far into dehumanizing the human race we choose to tread via endless population growth.

Thus, nothing gets solved while everything consequential happening to the planet accelerates. Therefore, Graham spelled it out in his quote: "...
but to absorb our global brothers and sisters until their horrid ordeal has been endured and shared by all—ten billion humans packed onto an ecologically devastated planet."

First world countries must ask themselves if they want to tread that path. Can the United States sustain the projected 100 million immigrants? Why should it? What will it mean to quality of life and standard of living for Americans? What will it mean as to water supplies and energy? Answer: it's all headed into the toilet faster than a bullet train.

From my world travels to all those places facing human chaos, I can unequivocally state that the United States, Canada, Europe and Australia stand on the edge of a demographic cliff. They cannot and will not save those developing world countries from their own fecundity follies, but, if they continue immigration without pause—those first world countries will surely sink into the abyss of the same conditions that the refugees fled.

At some point, the United States must take stock of its path. Can it decide its future? On the current path, can America withstand its impending demographic disaster? Do Americans understand they face a mathematical certainty? Do Americans realize it's only a matter of time? Do you dear reader understand the gravity, immediacy and certainty of your children's calamitous future?

CHAPTER 7

//

NO SPECIES CAN GET AWAY WITH THIS

"Unlimited population growth cannot be sustained; you cannot sustain growth in the rates of consumption of resources. No species can overrun the carrying capacity of a finite land mass. This Law cannot be repealed and is not negotiable." Dr. Albert Bartlett, University of Colorado

The late Dr. Bartlett spoke around the world with his profoundly brilliant presentation: "Arithmetic, Population and Energy." He presented it to world leaders, our U.S. Congress and environmental organizations 1,600 times in 30 years. **No one acted upon his sobering facts.** You may access his "YouTube" presentation or visit his website to view the entire presentation. (Source: www.albartlett.org)

In his lecture, both humorous and sobering at the same time, Bartlett presented audiences with irrefutable science as to the end result of "exponential growth." We humans, thinking we enjoy some kind of dispensation from reality, or the Pope for that matter, continue adding 83 million of ourselves annually, net gain.

In 1963, America featured a manageable 194 million people. By 1970 with birth control, American women averaged 2.03 children each. We citizens chose to stabilize our population based on our water, energy, resources, quality of life and standard of living needs. Our population would have leveled out at 255 million by 1990. However, our U.S. Congress imported over 100 million immigrants with their subsequent children from 1965 to 2006. And the onslaught continues to this day.

In 2021, cities like Chicago, Los Angeles, Atlanta, Denver, New York, Houston and many more feature horrific traffic congestion, toxic air pollution, crippling environmental problems and loss of quality of life. Infrastructure crumbles, massive unemployment prevails, poverty swells, and illiteracy grows. Unfortunately, no one can figure out how to solve our enormous problems.

Nonetheless, Congress imports another 100,000 immigrants every 30 days. They arrive from already overloaded countries around the world. They, in turn, birth 900,000 babies annually. Thus, the United States adds, from population momentum, immigration and birthrates—3.1 million annually. (Source: U.S. Population Projections by Fogel/Martin, PEW Research Center, www.PewResearchCenter.org, Dr. Steven Camarota, "Immigrant Birthrates", www.cis.org)

Unlimited Population Growth Cannot Be Sustained

What did Dr. Bartlett mean by the statement: "Unlimited population growth cannot be sustained"? What does he mean by "exponential growth"?

Exponential growth means that some quantity grows by a fixed percentage rate from one year to the next. A handy formula for calculating the doubling time for exponential growth: a survey of Boulder, Colorado residents thought a rate of 10 percent per year was desirable.

Ten percent year may not seem innocuous but let's see how these numbers would add up:

- Year 1 equals 60,000
- Year 2 equals 66,000
- Year 3 equals 72,600
- Year 4 equals 79,860
- Year 5 equals 87,846
- Year 6 equals 96,630
- Year 7 equals 106,294
- Year 8 equals 116,923

So, in eight years, the population doubles and by then 10,000 new residents per year move to Boulder (or any city). Exponential growth, in general, is not understood by the public. If exponential use of a resource is not accounted for in planning—disaster will transpire, i.e., water shortages, energy depletion and resource exhaustion. **The difference between linear growth and exponential growth is astonishing.**

The residents of Easter Island, after they pursued exponential growth for decades, collapsed and caused the extinction of their entire civilization. In other words, they ate themselves out of house and home. Every civilization faces the same fate if it continues exponential growth.

Unfortunately, in 2021, the United States heads down the exact same path as Easter Island. Grow, grow, grow! No Plan A, no Plan B, no reasonable understanding of its predicament! A small percentage of power elites that lead our country, lack any conceptual understanding of "exponential growth." Thus, they encourage ever greater population expansion. Millions of American citizens ride in the same boat and espouse endless population growth—as if the problems we already face can be solved by such arrogance and stupidity.

Dr. Bartlett also said, "Can you think of any problem in any area of human endeavor on any scale, from microscopic to global, whose long-term solution is in any demonstrable way aided, assisted, or advanced by further increases of population, locally, nationally, or globally?"

Can we clear up the toxic brown clouds hovering above our cities by adding more people, more cars and more exhaust chimneys to those cities? Can we solve the acid rain or acidification of our oceans by adding more people, homes and cars? Can we create more fresh water for the seven states now experiencing droughts and low water supplies by doubling their populations?

Georgia and Florida already suffer water shortages, yet expect to double their populations by mid-century. We cannot grow more food while each added American destroys 25.4 acres of arable land. We're painting ourselves into a corner from which we will not be able to extricate ourselves. In other words, once that next 100 million refugees land on our shores, they become our quandary. At some point, we will not be able to solve that problem. As their numbers grow within our country beyond our carrying capacity, we Americans become their victims. (Source: www.allspecies.org)

Why are we humans doing this to ourselves? Why do we pursue "exponential growth" with a vengeance? When will our citizens speak up and force our leaders to address human overpopulation in America and around the world?

Dr. Bartlett said, "No species can overrun the carrying capacity of a finite land mass. This Law cannot be repealed and is not negotiable."

So, what are we doing to ourselves as a species? At present, we race along making a pact with the "devil" in what we call a Faustian Bargain or, we keep adding people and burning up our resources for the luxury of the moment; as if tomorrow will never come. When tomorrow eventually arrives, we face Hobson's Choice. You won't like his choice! We will have exacerbated our situation to the point that only two choices remain available: we get to choose Door A which, when we step through it, we plummet over a cliff. Door B allows us to fall into quicksand with no lifeguards. In other words, our civilization faces collapse and we're all screwed with no choices.

As Dr. Bartlett said, **"The law cannot be repealed and is not negotiable." The Law of Gravity gives you an idea of what it's like to fall over a cliff with no parachute. At some point, the United States faces the inevitable consequences of "exponential growth."**

Shouldn't we be listening and taking action to avert the consequences?

CHAPTER 8

///

OIL ENABLED A 100-YEAR WINDOW THAT'S CLOSING

"The cheap oil age created an artificial bubble of plentitude for a period not much longer than a human lifetime....so I hazard to assert that as oil ceases to be cheap and the world reserves move toward depletion, we will be left with an enormous population...that the ecology of the earth will not support. The journey back toward non-oil population homeostasis will not be pretty. We will discover the hard way that population hyper-growth was simply a side-effect of the oil age. It was a condition, not a problem with a solution. That is what happened, and we are stuck with it." James Howard Kunstler, The Long Emergency

Top experts around the world understand that the energy slave called "oil" faces exhaustion within the next 29 years, if not sooner. Along the way, drilling for oil will prove more difficult, harder to extract and more costly.

Fact: everything in America and most Western civilizations runs on oil. Oil allows billions of people to eat via tractors and harvesters of massive croplands. You've heard of the 3,000 mile fruit salad you're enjoying, right? The fruits arrived from Chile with virgin olive oil from Italy and pineapples from Mexico. A plane or truck hauled them to your grocery store. You drove down to pick up your salad fixings.

Without oil, 330 million Americans could not feed themselves and 7.8 billion humans around the planet would face enormous die-off. We humans cannot possibly plant and harvest enough food by hand to survive for THAT many people. We couldn't pump the aquifers to irrigate crops. We couldn't transport food fast enough by boat, donkey or oxen.

That's the problem. Oil will be exhausted by mid-century, or what might be described as a blink of an eye! Nothing on the technological horizon can replace it. When you multiply 365 days by 99 million barrels of oil burned daily, it equals to more than a cubic mile of oil!

In his book, **The Long Emergency,** Kunstler discovered that China, at its current growth rate and placing 27,000 new cars on its highways every week, will burn 98 million barrels of oil per day by 2030. That's the amount the world burns daily in 2021. That means a whole lot of human beings will be screwed when oil supplies dry up.

Along this fossil fuel burning path, we create enormous carbon footprint overloading our biosphere. Acid rain destroys soil-nitrogen balance. In other words, it's going to get ugly worldwide on multiple fronts. In realty, with all the chemicals injected into the soil, sprayed over the fields and painted onto those crops—it already is more than ugly for the pollinators—the lifeblood of our planet.

If you remember your science, it took 2.0 billion years to produce all the oil on this planet. In other words, when oil reserves decline, we exhaust the single major energy source that drives our civilization and most other societies on this planet.

Alternative Energy Won't Save Humanity

To show how much energy oil provides the U.S. annually, Michael Brownlee of Transition Boulder County provided an astounding graph of one cubic mile of oil. That's how much oil humans burn around the planet each year!

That equals to the same amount of energy provided by 52 nuclear power plants built every year for 50 years. Or, 104 operating coal-fired electrical plants built every year for 50 years. Or, 32,000 wind turbines built every year for 50 years—and in continuous operation. Or, 91,250,000 solar panels built every year for 50 years.

(Source: www.transitionbouldercounty.org)

In other words, oil produces dramatically incredible amounts of energy that we cannot and will not be able to duplicate in the coming years.

A friend of mine asked, "How many is twenty million?"

In this age of millions, billions and trillions, it's hard to understand such numbers. Twenty million is the number of barrels of oil we burn in the United States each day.

That's 42 gallons to each barrel (drum) at 30 inches tall and 20 inches in diameter, or 840,000,000 gallons burned per day. It calculates, to three gallons of oil per day per person in the USA.

Suppose we took 20 million barrels and stood them side-by-side. How long a line of barrels would that make? Let's do the math: 20 inches/barrel multiplied by 20 million barrels equals 400,000,000 inches. Divide that by 12 inches/foot, and you get 33,333,333 feet. Divide that by 5,280 feet per mile, and that comes out to 6,313 miles.

Let's compute a string of barrels reaching from Seattle to Los Angeles (1,157 miles), from Los Angeles to Chicago (2,134 miles), from Chicago to Miami (1,377 miles), from Miami to New York City (1,281 miles), and from New York City to Cleveland (486 miles). Total mileage, 6,435!

That's how much oil we burn in the USA each day. The total global consumption daily rate of 99 million would be four times this amount, or 25,000 miles—the circumference of the globe at the equator!

How much longer can this go on? The simple, unadulterated answer is: not much longer! You may want to read, ***Out of Gas: The End of the Age of Oil*** by David Goodstein, physics professor at California Institute of Technology.

Imagine millions upon millions of miles of highways loaded with cars all burning gasoline and diesel 24/7. Imagine you breathe all that polluted air. Imagine what it will be like when America adds another 100, 200 and 300 million more people and cars. Imagine how the planet will react to another 2.2 billion more people burning fossil fuels by 2050. Are you sick yet? What about your children?

Another scientist, Dr. Richard C. Duncan, introduced the **Olduvai Theory:** ***The Peak of World Oil Production and the Road to the Olduvai Gorge.***

The decline of the industrial civilization is broken into three sections:

- The Olduvai slope (1979–1999)—Energy per capita declined at 0.33 percent per year.
- The Olduvai slide (2000–2011)—Begins in 2000 with the escalating warfare in the Middle East... marks the all-time peak of world oil production.
- The Olduvai cliff (2012–2030)—Begins in 2012 when an epidemic of permanent blackouts spread worldwide, i.e., first there are waves of brownouts and temporary blackouts, and then finally the electric power networks themselves expire.

Americans wear out nearly 300 million tires annually. We throw them into huge dumps or burn them into the atmosphere. Imagine another 100, 200 and 300 million added Americans burning all that oil and burning up all those tires. Ever wonder what Mother Nature plans for us with all this abuse?

"We will discover the hard way that population hyper-growth was simply a side-effect of the oil age," said Kunstler.

Instead of learning a very harsh lesson bearing down on our society like a brakeless freight train, what can you do? As you become more educated and sobered to America's population predicament, the logical question jumps up in front of your face: what can I do to help change course?

CHAPTER 9

//

WE NEED TO THINK LIKE A LIFE-GIVING PLANET

"The world has set in motion environmental trends that are threatening civilization itself. We are crossing environmental thresholds and violating deadlines set by nature. Nature is the timekeeper, but we cannot see the clock." Lester Brown, Plan B 4.0 Saving Civilization

We human beings prove to be the most aberrant species ever evolved on planet Earth. Within 100 years, we transformed this green, ecologically balanced and thriving globe into an environmental nightmare. We created the "Sixth Extinction Session" whereby 100 plus species suffer extinction every single day of the year. We pump our fossil fuel carbon exhaust into the biosphere at such a rate of speed that our pollution acidifies the soils and oceans of the world.

Our poisoning of the biosphere's air creates acid rain that falls upon forests, lakes and streams—wiping out their "pH" balance that subsequently kills other creatures, both plant and animal, indiscriminately. Our deadly, filthy injection of 84,000 human-made chemicals into the air, land and water 24/7 unwinds the very foundation of life-based DNA on this planet. Our Genetically Modified Organisms create an insurmountable and growing nightmare for Mother Nature.

We poisoned the foundation of our marine food supply with radioactive waste like Fukushima reactors exploding and pouring billions of gallons of deadly waste into the Pacific. Virtually all rivers such as the Mississippi, Yangtze, Ganges, Seine and others dump trillions of gallons of chemical waste 24/7.

By the way, the Mississippi River features a 10,000 square mile dead zone because it spews endless toxic chemicals into the Gulf of Mexico 24/7. So, no, we Americans aren't any more environmentally responsible than the Chinese or Indians.

As clever as we prove ourselves to be, we cannot imagine the catastrophic trends we set in motion by tinkering with Nature's internal systems. To think that our actions will not be met with responses—proves the height of arrogance for our species.

Already, massive die-off in our oceans as to sharks, whales, reefs and other marine life threaten the delicate balance of life on Earth. Our carbon footprint usurps our weather patterns to create "Katabatic" hurricanes like Katrina and Sandy. (Source: www.350.org)

Consider the Great Pacific Garbage Patch:

Journalist Lindsey Hoshaw said, "Light bulbs, bottle caps, toothbrushes, popsicle sticks, soda pop plastic bottles, water bottles and tiny pieces of plastic, each the size of a grain of rice, inhabit the Pacific garbage patch, an area of widely dispersed trash that doubles in size every decade and is now believed to be roughly twice the size of Texas. But one research organization estimates that the garbage now pervades the Pacific, though most of it is caught in a gyre — an area of heavy currents and slack winds that keep the trash swirling in a giant whirlpool."

Pipes drain chemicals into the oceans from countries all over the world. Poisoning of our oceans means poisoning of our marine life, plants and ultimately all of us. Today, a pregnant woman is advised NOT to eat more than one helping of tuna or salmon per month due to ill effects upon her fetus.

In his book, **Plan B 4.0 Saving Civilization,** Lester Brown said, "The thinking that got us into this mess is not likely to get us out. We need a new mindset. Let me paraphrase a comment by environmentalist Paul Hawken, 'In recognizing the enormity of the challenge facing us,' he said: 'First we need to decide what needs to be done. And then we ask if it is possible. Then, we do it.'"

Having scuba dived all over the planet in the past 58 years, I can attest that the oceans enjoyed pristine beauty up until 1965 before plastics, but today, our oceans roll in junk, plastic, metal cans, glass, tires and trash from countless military, luxury cruise ships and pleasure crafts tossing their refuse without end. Our military forces around the world use the oceans for a final toilet of chemicals. Mustard gas, radioactive wastes and the 84,000 chemicals we have created flow for a final resting place into our oceans.

Lester Brown speaks about the enormous consequences of adding population, "The first trend of concern is population growth. Each year there are 83 million more people at the dinner table. Unfortunately, the overwhelming majority of these individuals are being added in countries where soils are eroding, water tables are falling, and irrigation wells are going dry. If we cannot get the brakes on population growth, we won't be able to eradicate hunger."

Imagine the starvation rates with the projected addition of 2.2 billion people by 2050. As human population explodes, arable land and water diminish. At some point, as Brown describes in his book, our numbers collide with the lack of water and food scarcity.

And yet, with that knowledge, humanity keeps accelerating its growth. No one wants, seems or cares to understand our predicaments. The science stares into our faces. The evidence crushes us with millions of humans suffering annually. The extinction rates of other creatures intensify.

Nonetheless, we continue our prolific fecundity without reason, without comprehension, and without thought.

As Brown addresses in his book, he makes the point that world militaries spend $1 trillion annually. Why not spend $100 billion on his **Plan B 4.0 Saving Civilization**?

He said, "The choice is ours—yours and mine. We can stay with business as usual and preside over an economy that continues to destroy its natural support systems until it destroys itself, or we can adopt Plan B and be the generation that changes direction, moving the world onto a path of sustained progress."

Fellow humans that care about the future; we need to start thinking like a planet. We can stop plastic debris by creating 50-cent deposit-return international laws on all plastic leaving commercial stores. We can stop injecting 84,000 chemicals 24/7 by mandating laws to stop producing them. We can stop human overpopulation by educating for birth control.

We can form international conferences to address human population overload and how to stop it. We can change course by using our brains, ideas and actions. Otherwise, Mother Nature bats last and she doesn't give a crap how many humans she takes out as she romps around the bases.

CHAPTER 10

EXPONENTIAL POPULATION GROWTH INVITES THE FOUR HORSEMEN OF THE APOCALYPSE

"The green revolution has won a temporary success in man's war against hunger and deprivation; it has given humanity a breathing space. If fully implemented, the revolution can provide sufficient food for sustenance during the next three decades. But the frightening power of human reproduction must also be curbed; otherwise, the success of the green revolution will be ephemeral only." Norman Borlaug, while accepting the Nobel Prize for peace in 1970

Ironically, Borlaug, not only foresaw mass human starvation, he unwittingly contributed to it. While his scientific experimenting with crops yielded greater gains per acre, he facilitated massive population growth that exploded the world from 3.5 billion in 1970 to our enormously hungry and thirsty 7.8 billion humans in the 21st century.

Despite Borlaug's efforts, he unwittingly created greater human starvation levels into the billions when the ax finally falls in the 21st century as to water, arable land and energy availability. **This fact remains: the ax will fall upon humanity in this century.**

Dreadful, miserable and deadly! Today, we humans seem to think we can outsmart Mother Nature. We can vanquish her! As you see in this graphic book, at this point, we seem to be winning. Oh contrare' fellow human! Not much longer!

For millions of years, Mother Nature culled any species that overwhelmed its carrying capacity of water, food and resources. When we humans came onto the scene, our cleverness allowed us a small niche which became a larger niche and today, homo erectus meaning "clever ape", rages across the planet with a self-evident arrogance that we can brutalize nature in any way we choose. We think we can poison the air, water and land without harm to ourselves. We think we can encroach on the rest of the natural world and kill off endless species—yet remain unharmed and untouched by our folly.

Think again!

Today in America, one out of six citizens suffers hunger. (Source: www.FeedingAmerica.org)

Poverty in America:

- In 2011, 46.2 million people (15.0 percent) lived in poverty.
- In 2011, 9.5 million (11.8 percent) families lived in poverty.
- In 2011, 26.5 million (13.7 percent) of people ages 18-64 lived in poverty.
- In 2011, 16.1 million (22.0 percent) children under the age of 18 lived in poverty.
- In 2011, 3.6 million (9.0 percent) seniors 65 and older lived in poverty.
- (It's much worse in 2021)

Food Insecurity and Very Low Food Security

- In 2011, 50.1 million Americans lived in food insecure households, 3.5 million adults and 16.7 million children.

These figures sober any American, but they do not begin to tell the story of 21st century world starvation dynamics. With our paltry 330 million human population, we also suffer the highest obesity rates in the world with over 60 percent of our citizens overweight and suffering from heart disease, diabetes and other medical health issues. But we also feature 40 + million Americans subsisting in food kitchens and food banks. An astounding 38 million Americans live off food stamps or today's Electronic Benefits Transfer credit cards. (EBT cards) (19)

"Children are the most visible victims of under-nutrition. Children who are poorly nourished suffer up to 160 days of illness each year. Poor nutrition plays a role in at least half of the 10 million child deaths each year—five million adult deaths." (Source: www.worldhunger.org)

How will our civilization survive the raging Four Horsemen of the Apocalypse? At the moment, we charge right into their cross hairs.

First, we need a national discussion-debate. We need to throw "population overload" onto the table. We need to come up with an "American Population Stabilization Policy" of two children or less per female. We need to stop mass immigration. In the very near future, we Americans need to encourage one-child per woman to overcome "population momentum" now eating up India and China. We need to be realistic and rational instead of emotional and religious. We cannot hope for good to ensue; we must act in order to create a viable civilization. This book applies to Canada, UK, Europe, New Zealand, Australia and most other countries of the world.

Without our immediate actions, we most certainly will become victims of the Four Horsemen of the Apocalypse.

As Borlaug said, "**But the frightening power of human reproduction must also be curbed; otherwise, the success of the green revolution will be ephemeral only.**"

CHAPTER II

///

GRIDLOCKED TRAFFIC WORLDWIDE

"A society sufficiently sophisticated to produce the internal combustion engine has not had the sophistication to develop cheap and efficient public transport. There are hardly any buses, the trains are hopelessly underfunded and hence, the entire population is stuck in traffic." Ben Elton, Gridlock

"Gridlocked traffic causes more deaths, more tension, more suffering and more emotional misery than yet understood. It defeats the human spirit with endless failure of the ability to move forward. You can be killed or maimed at any moment by another automobile. Drivers fume in their seats while their cars fume-up the biosphere. Gridlocked traffic worsens by the year as humanity grows its collective population by 83 million annually. Gridlocked traffic can never be solved as long as humans refuse to address the root cause of the problem." FHW

From my own experiences in traffic in Hong Kong, Tokyo, Sao Paulo, Sydney, Houston, Paris, New York, Los Angeles, Chicago, Denver, Atlanta, Beijing, Shanghai, Atlanta, San Francisco and dozens of other overpopulated cities, we've got enormous traffic problems all over the globe.

America's gridlocked traffic worsens annually because our country adds 3.1 million more people to the mix year in and year out, decade in and decade out. More people equal more cars, which means more exhaust, which means more toxic-polluted air with every breath, which means more asthma, which means more lung cancer and the Brown Cloud over our cities grows without pause.

An average of 35,000 to 40,000 Americans lose their lives every year in traffic crashes. In Denver, Colorado where I live, gridlocked traffic accounts for 20 to 30 crashes every day of the work week. To put Denver's traffic into a few words: an exasperating daily living nightmare.

Millions of drivers drive drunk 24/7 on America's highways. You might go to work one morning and suffer an auto crash that takes your life or places you in the ICU at your local hospital. Mothers Against Drunk Driver researched alcoholic drivers at 14 million of them 24/7 driving on America's highways.

According to the USA National Highway Traffic Administration, car accidents occur every minute of the day: "Motor vehicle accidents occur in any part of the world every 60 seconds. And if it's all summed up in a yearly basis, there are **5.15 million driving accidents** that take place annually in the USA. Statistics show that each year, 35,000 of the United States' population die due to vehicular accidents and around 2.9 million people end up suffering light or severe injuries. It is also affirmed that car accidents kill a child every three minutes."

Not only do all those cars exhaust their carbon particles into the biosphere 24/7, but look at the mega-buildings with millions of smokestacks pouring toxic filth into the air endlessly. I have traveled through China and they plunge so far into the Dante's Environmental Inferno that the only thing they can do is suffer, die and degrade their environment into submission.

Canada Free Press reported, "Here's one way to get attention: traffic deaths worldwide kill the equivalent number of people as would perish in nine jumbo jet crashes every day. World traffic injuries are taking the lives of 145 people every hour of every day (totaling 3,500 per day). This is more than two a minute and adds up to 1.3 million people dying on the world's roads each year and a further 20 million people suffering injuries, often debilitating ones."

Already in China where they push 27,000 new cars onto their highways every single week of the year, some 27 million cars added annually as reported by NBC's Lester Holt, they suffer unimaginable gridlock. China features one of the longest gridlocked traffic fiascos in modern history at

62 miles long gridlock traffic jam that took 12 days to resolve. Motorists ran out of gas, out of water and out of food while stuck in traffic.

http://www.popsci.com/science/article/2010-08/62-mile-nine-day-traffic-jam-spells-disaster-commuter-promise-chinas-auto-industry

Multiple car crashes involve 20 to 50 vehicles and more as drivers rush toward their destinations in rain, fog, snow and overloaded highways.

Why won't global leaders meet in a world conference to deal with the environmental, social and mega-city consequences we humans created around the planet? When we see such enormous traffic gridlock, why do we think building more roads, highways and expressways will solve the problem? It won't, it can't, and it doesn't.

How can Los Angeles solve its God-awful and God-forsaken gridlock by adding another 10 million people, which demographic experts predict before 2050? What kinds of minds think they can solve anything by growing it bigger?

Einstein said, "The problems in the world today are so enormous, they cannot be solved with the level of thinking that created them."

Humans and vehicles fare poorly in auto collisions that occur every minute of every day around the globe. The human misery, loss and suffering from these crashes cannot be measured. As the human race gallops toward an added 2.2 billion more people by 2050, human car-crash deaths will skyrocket from their already horrific numbers in 2021.

I have personally traveled through most of the major overpopulated cities in the world. It's like trying to wrestle a giant squid with one foot. It's like trying to fly using toothpicks for wings. It's like trying to run with 100 pound weights attached to your ankles. You get the picture!

So, what's the answer? Demographic expert Jason Brent of Los Vegas, Nevada spelled it out: "Therefore, the only problem, the ultimate problem, facing humanity is to reduce our population as quickly as possible with the least amount of death and destruction, and to determine who will be permitted to reproduce when the population contraction commences in the very near future. Compared to the problem described above every other problem faced by humanity is irrelevant and unimportant. If the problem described above is not solved, billions will die due to the decline in economic activity which will cause continuous wars and other horrors until the population is reduced to the level the declining economic activity can support."

As our civilization adds another 100 million people driving cars by mid-century, what's your solution?

CHAPTER 12

OCEANS OF PLASTIC, PLASTIC FISH

"Plastics prove the worst, most insidious invention of humanity. Plastics kill everything and anything in their path on all four corners of the planet. Plastics kill without violence, without warning and without provocation. Plastics float, sink and never break down. Of all of humanity's follies on this green planet, plastics take the trophy for man's inhumanity to all other life forms and eco-systems on Earth." FHW

Plastic Onslaught in an Ocean of Grief

This chapter cannot help but appall your sense of humanity's moral and ethical decay on this planet. Not to mention its outright denial of reality! This plastic onslaught stands alone as the worst invasion ever perpetrated on all other creatures on Earth. While I respond to many religiously righteous people and many people who think they know what they are talking about—I am chagrined at the arrogance of those who defend unlimited human growth in the face of our accelerating carnage, slaughter and butchery of the Natural World around the planet.

Marco Torres, March 26, 2013, wrote in Prevent Disease:

"Overpopulation is a radical and dangerous myth promoted by elite and international societies. The unproven notion, as Malthus believed, that higher wages and welfare should be withheld from the great unwashed because he believed that these two factors would allow the poor to survive and exponentially breed, thus compounding the overpopulation problem. Overpopulation is a misnomer. A problem that exists only in dramatically erroneous theories that are not mathematically based. It is simply one of the most flawed concepts right up there with global warming. The theories are based on myths, not science or accurate statistical correlations or causation principles."

(Source: www.PreventDisease.com)

In reality, Malthus said, *"The power of population is so superior to the power of earth to produce subsistence to humanity that premature death must in some shape or other visit the human race."*

Those of us that possess greater understanding can only shake our heads at the insanity of humanity's folly. To take Malthus several steps further into the accelerating nightmare of overpopulation on this planet—let us address the 84,000 human-made chemicals our species injects into the land, air and water 24/7. How does Torres speak to that nasty reality? Answer: he ignores it. How about the most insidious aspect of humanity's inventions—plastics? Torres ducks out along with all pro-growth advocates. They never deal with the undercurrent of human devastation on this planet.

Reports state that 5.25 trillion pieces of plastic float or sink in all the oceans of the world. Those pieces of plastic may be the size of a pin head (nurdles) or the length of a football field as in drift nets. They kill when eaten or they kill when fed to youngsters. They kill with no mercy and they kill 24/7. Plastics prove themselves "The Perfect Extinction Machine." The invention of plastics attest to humanity's greatest curse upon the Natural World.

This chapter may distress you more than usual. The 10-minute video below illustrates the deadly reach of humanity as its plastics attack the bird life on Midway Island, seemingly so far away from human encroachment, that such an onslaught of human-made rubbish couldn't reach it. But it does, and the avian and marine life suffer excruciating deaths from having their guts loaded with every form of plastic tossed into the oceans without any responsibility whatsoever. It's titled: **An Ocean of Grief** on YouTube:

https://www.facebook.com/photo.php?v=10151444416028934&set=vb.121736167844852&type=2&theater

Now that you've seen this painful video of our disregard of the Natural World, how do we account for ourselves as a species? How do we change this ugly, nasty and deadly assault on Mother Nature?

You saw the lethal plastics invading the guts of the birds, but what about below the ocean waves? Let me tell you with my 58 years of scuba diving around the planet, it's even more deadly. We kill off 100 million sharks annually for the past 30 years—documented by Julia Whitty in One Earth Magazine. Also, in Life Magazine, 1990 issue! The carnage below the water equals everything and more above the water.

Golf balls found in the ocean and the rest of the detritus represents a tiny, tiny fraction of the amount of plastic debris discarded into our oceans and washed up on shore. It will take millions of years after the human race departs the planet for all our crap to degrade. In the meantime, it will continue killing millions of unsuspecting marine creatures as well as wipe-out countless species.

Sea turtles eat Styrofoam so much so—they cannot submerge to find their food. Dolphins and whales get caught up in drift nets to the point of strangulation, suffocation and agonizing deaths. Researchers regularly discover 100 pounds of plastics in dead whales that washed up upon the shoreline. The tiny plastic pellets (nurdles) by the billions upon billions now infect the ocean food chain. Even that horror cannot be seen in the film, but it operates everywhere in the oceans.

Almost 25 years ago, the popular TV talk show host Oprah Winfrey exposed the 100-million-ton plastic floating garbage patch the size of Texas desecrating an area of the Pacific Ocean. The "Great Pacific Garbage Patch" covers all other oceans of the world with an average of 46,000 plastic bottles and debris floating on every square mile of ocean water. That plastic kills millions of creatures above and below the surface.

Did the world media come to the rescue? Did the president of the United States and leaders of all other countries in the world call for a world 50-cent deposit/return law to stop this deluge of plastics entering our Natural World? Did ordinary citizens take action to make it happen in free countries? Did Pepsi, Coke, Coors, Budweiser, Kentucky Bourbon, KFC, McDonald's, Burger King, Chipotle's, Pizza Hut, Toys-R-US and other top beverage and plastic-selling companies stand up to demand deposit/return laws for all their products. Did CEO's of Ford, Chrysler,

General Motors, Kroger, Publix, King Soopers, Coors, and Safeway make any attempt to stop plastics from entering the natural world?

Answer: not a single, pathetic one of them stood up to promote a plan to stop the destruction of our oceans. In fact, I know one of them personally, Peter Coors of Coors Brewing in Golden, Colorado where I live. He used his millions of dollars to defeat container-deposit laws in Colorado in 1974 and 1988. I asked him why? He said to me in a letter, "It's only an eight percent waste stream…."

When you take eight percent, and apply it to trillions of plastic containers, you come up with the "Great Pacific Garbage Patch." I call Peter Coors a "pretend environmentalist."

In third world countries, people toss everything as if they still lived in the Stone Age. They walk in it, through it and throw more into it. Don't laugh: Americans, Canadians, Europeans and Australians all toss their trash into the oceans, along roadsides, in parks, in rivers, in lakes and into streams. The human race as a whole proves itself dangerously clueless.

Thus, the onslaught of our oceans rips at the foundation of all of life. And guys like Marco Torres insist that human overpopulation remains a myth, a charade and a misnomer. To that, I conclude Torres continues breathing but remains "an intellectually vacant parking lot."

CHAPTER 13

///

ROOT CAUSE OF HUMANITY'S PREDICAMENT

"One can see from space how the human race has changed the Earth. Nearly all of the available land has been cleared of forests and is now used for agriculture or urban development. The polar icecaps are shrinking, and the desert areas are increasing. At night, the Earth is no longer dark, but large areas are lit up. All of this is evidence that human exploitation of the planet is reaching a critical limit. But human demands and expectations are ever-increasing. We cannot continue to pollute the atmosphere, poison the ocean and exhaust the land. There isn't any more available."

Stephen Hawking, Physicist & Author

Why would Hawking make such a profound statement as you read above if he didn't understand our predicament as to human overpopulation? An even better question: why haven't the leaders of the world responded? How about the religions of the world? How about ordinary citizens of the world already suffering by several billion via the onslaught of overpopulation? Answer: mass denial, illiteracy, religious insanity and greed.

This year, in 2021, millions of adults and children face starvation, which occurs every year, year after year, decade after decade.

With all the intelligence and understanding we possess, not one world leader addresses the starvation rates or the magnitude of the population explosion.

Africans must trudge three to four miles to pick up water in many areas. They starve to death by the tens of thousands, yet they continue on course from their current 1.3 billion people to reach 2.0 billion by 2050 and 4.0 billion by the end of this century.

Let's discuss water: every 21 seconds, a child dies from water related diseases. More than 3.4 million people die each year from water, sanitation, and hygiene-related causes. Nearly 99 percent of all deaths occur in the developing world. Lack of access to clean water and sanitation kills children at a rate equivalent of a jumbo jet crashing every four hours. Of the 60 million people added to the world's towns and cities every year, most move to informal settlements (i.e., slums) with no sanitation facilities. Over 780 million people lack access to an improved water source: approximately one in nine people. (20)

An American taking a five-minute shower uses more water than the average person in a developing country slum uses for an entire day. An American uses 101 gallons of water 24/7. A developing world person uses five gallons or less, daily. (21) (Source: www.water.org)

Religious irrationality: let's talk about the Catholic Church, Islam, Hindus and all the other ancient religions that fight against birth control. With all the misery exploding in countries around the world, the Pope refuses to step into the 21st century and advocate for birth control. His troglodyte mind cannot advance to logical and rational thinking for taking action in the 21st century. He fosters human misery on a scale not seen in all of history. He represents "religious irrationality." Same for Islam, Hindus and the rest of the myopic religions of the world!

Illiteracy: let's talk about what drives such fecundity rates. While they starve in refugee camps in Africa, women average 8.2 kids during their fertile years. Muslims, Christians and other tribal people birth more kids than "Toys-R-Us" can produce plastic tricycles. Illiteracy begets more children, and more children beget more starvation, and more starvation creates an endless cycle of human misery not comprehended in the Western world. Ironically, those humanitarian "Feed the Children" programs beg for money to feed those kids. The more they feed their numbers, the greater their numbers. Noble, but imprudent! Why? Answer: the more you feed starving people, the more they reproduce beyond their carrying capacity, which means they end up starving in greater numbers.

Most Westerners lack any comprehension of the human misery facing over 2.0 billion humans on this planet that cannot find enough food and water each day.

Greed: nothing like capitalism and other forms of perpetual growth systems that support ceaseless escalation on every level. Heads of corporations refuse to deal with reality, the facts or anything that denies them more production, more products, more consumption, more plastic, more money and more power. Pretty sickening, actually. Mother Nature doesn't stand a chance against such human greed. At least, not for the moment—in the end she always bats last, i.e., hurricanes Katrina, Sandy, earthquakes, deserts, starvation, and diseases.

"Over-consumption and overpopulation underlie every environmental problem we face today." Jacques-Yves Cousteau, Oceanographer

Cousteau nailed it, but we continue to ignore that wise man. We need to take action to change the underlying cause of most of the planet's exploding environmental, chemical, extinction and related problems.

Lack of water in the United States at some point will become the cause of much conflict as America currently suffers seven states in water shortages and more to come. This picture will become our picture at some point.

Dr. Jack Alpert, Stanford University said: "There are many experts in the world. Each, from his or her area of expertise (soil, water, energy, biodiversity, waste impacts, food, conflict, minerals, metals) reports degradation, exhaustion and civilization disruption. The collective human needs of 7.8 billion people are bigger than the earth's production. Call this overshoot. Overshoot exists even if human footprint does not expand. When, for example, fossil energy diminishes overshoot increases." (Source: www.Skil.org)

Here Is What We Face

In the Natural World, overshoot generates collapse. Too many wolves for the available caribou and the wolf population dies back. We humans are little different from wolves. On the upside we have technology that might obtain more from less. On the downside, each human unequally consumes resources. The "haves" in first world countries consume many times the "have nots" in developing countries. As the scarcity continues to increase (because soil is lost, land inundated, weather changes, energy deliveries become exhausted by 2050) the haves will consume the food that fed "have nots."

The have nots will starve or fight to survive. The social conflict will engulf everyone by 2050. By the end of this century, after we have squandered our one-time bounty of resources, less than 500 million people will be living at subsistence levels. (Source: Dr. Jack Alpert, www.skil.org)

That is not a good plan. It is the result of our current course. Our solution is almost like that of the wolves. The strong survive. Or the strong quickly kill off the weak so the existing caribou can support them.

"Humans have an additional alternative," Alpert said. "We can stop having babies until our population declines enough to be supported by earth."

CHAPTER 14

KILLING BEES IN AMERICA AND WORLDWIDE WILL BE THE DEATH OF HUMANITY

"If all mankind were to disappear, the world would regenerate back to the rich state of equilibrium that existed ten thousand years ago. If insects were to vanish, the environment would collapse into chaos."
Harvard University biologist Edward O. Wilson

Humanity's devastation by poisoning of bees will be the death of all humankind

Each day, millions of Americans across this country spray Roundup, Weed-Be-Gone, Termite Spray, Bug Killer, Wasp Spray and hundreds of other poisons onto their sidewalks, driveways, bushes, trees, flowers and onto their lawns. They kill everything that pecks, slithers, crawls, flaps, bites and breathes. Their mass slaughter includes bats, honeybees, flies, butterflies, mosquitoes, wasps, bumblebees and other pollinators. Billions upon trillions of insects suffer death via poisons that disrupt their breathing or digestive tracks. Trillions more die on the front bumpers of cars, trucks, trains and planes.

As human life menacingly expands across the planet, it devours the Natural World. It kills the balance of the Natural World. It murders just about anything that flies, swims, runs, bites or burps. According to a High Country News report years ago, Americans kill one vertebrate animal crossing our roads (roadkill) every 11.5 seconds. That equals to one million deaths every day of the year. That equals 365 million creatures that lose their lives to tires, boat propellers, fans, combines, mowing machines, jet intakes, aircraft propellers and other mechanical devices every year. Note: that study did not include the rest of the world. Humans kill everything that runs, leaps, flies or swims—by the billions and trillions. The number of insects that die annually on the hoods of cars and trucks must be in the endless-trillions. (25) (Source: www.HighCountryNews.com)

But we shall pay for our transgressions when it comes to the pollinators: bees, bats, wasps, butterflies and other insects.

Consider the coming collapse of the $30 billion honeybee economy in the US.

"Since 2006 honeybees responsible for pollinating more than 100 crops—from apples to zucchini—have been dying by the tens of millions," said a Huffington Post report. "As a new report from the US Department of Agriculture (USDA) details, scientists are still struggling to pinpoint the cause of so-called Colony Collapse Disorder (CCD) and time is running out. The survivorship of honeybee colonies is too low for us to be confident in our ability to meet the pollination demands of U.S. agricultural crops."

The CCD has wiped out some 10 million beehives worth $2 billion over the past six years. The death rate for colonies has hit 30 percent annually in recent years and there are now about 2.5 million honeybee colonies in the U.S., down from six million in 1947 and three million in 1990. That downward spiral leaves "virtually no cushion of bees for pollination.

"With mounting information, it becomes downright frightening," said USDA scientist Jeff Pettis. "For example: take almonds. California harvests more than 80 percent of the world's almonds. But you can't grow the nut without honeybees, and it takes 60 percent of the U.S.'s remaining colonies to pollinate that $4 billion cash crop."

If the death toll continues at the present rate, that means there will soon be barely enough bees to pollinate almonds, let alone avocados, blueberries, pears or plums.

"We are one poor weather event or high winter bee loss away from a pollination disaster,'" said Jeff Pettis.

Jacques Cousteau worried about what humans were doing to the ecosystem: ***"If we go on the way we have, the fault is our greed and if we are not willing to change, we will disappear from the face of the globe to be replaced by the insect."***

Scientists report several factors—from disease-carrying parasites to pesticides. What sickens me stems from the fact that we know our chemicals disrupt every living creature in a cornfield, wheatfield, potato field, tomato patch, soy and bean acre. Yet we pour, spray and inject more and more poisons.

A beekeeper in California said, "Bees are vital to our lives as they are among the primary pollinators of our food plants. It has been deduced that if our native bees were to die out the effect on crops and wildflowers would be utterly catastrophic. As these crops and flowers provide food for our wild and farm animals, we could easily lose up to a third of our regular diet. This is a very real problem, and one that is not getting the attention it needs."

Bees and other pollinators allow humanity to thrive. Without them, we won't survive the 21st century. It's particularly galling, if not a whole new dimension of stupid, for our species to continue expanding our numbers while we diminish insect numbers, rodent numbers, big beasts and avian numbers at a rate of one-million daily via roadkill in the USA alone. Please realize that the High Country News report featured only the 48 lower states. When you look worldwide at roadkill rates in India, China, Mexico, Australia, Europe, Canada, Indochina and most other countries that feature millions of vehicles—the death rates must scream off the charts.

It makes humans a "Monstrous Killing Machine" around the planet.

But the wholesale poisoning via such vicious herbicides like **Roundup** makes me sick to my stomach. Those poisons travel into the ground, into the angleworms, into the birds, into the bugs and finally into the water systems where they ultimately poison each and every one of us. How can we be this senseless?

We wonder why one out of three Americans suffers from the second biggest killer in the USA: cancer. How arrogant can we prove ourselves? How absolutely out of touch and in denial of reality can we be? What kind of intellectually and morally bankrupt, greedy, money-mongers make TV commercials parading **Roundup** to millions of uninformed Americans too lazy to bend down and pull out the weeds on their driveway with their hands?

To think that within another 29 years, our country will grow by 100 million Americans while the rest of the world adds another 2.2 billion people—all capable of using **Roundup** and hundreds of other poisons to kill the bees of the world. We prove ourselves to be the most clever— dumbest species on this planet.

Tama Janowitz puts the earthly competition between insects and humans this way: *"Long after the bomb falls and you and your good deeds are gone, cockroaches, will still be here, prowling the streets like armored cars."*

CHAPTER 15

//

COWS, HOGS, CHICKENS, FISH, CORPORATE & FAMILY FARMS

"Livestock are one of the most significant contributors to today's most serious environmental problems. Urgent action is required to remedy the situation." Henning Steinfeld, Chief of FAO's Livestock Information and Policy Branch

Enormous environmental destruction from raising domestic animals for consumption: Raising animals for slaughter, consumption and feed

According to a new report published by the United Nations Food and Agriculture Organization, the livestock sector generates more greenhouse gas emissions as measured in CO_2 equivalent – 18 percent – than transport. It is also a major source of land and water degradation.

As far as food is concerned, the great extravagance is not caviar or truffles, but beef, pork and poultry. Some 38 percent of the world's grain crop is now fed to animals, as well as large quantities of soybeans. There are three times as many domestic animals on this planet as there are human beings. (Source: United Nations Food and Agriculture Organization)

The combined weight of the world's 1.5 billion cattle alone exceeds that of the human population. While we look darkly at the number of babies being born in poorer parts of the world, we ignore the over-population of farm animals, to which we contribute. That, however, is only part of the damage done by the animals we breed.

"The energy intensive factory farming methods of the industrialized nations are responsible for the consumption of huge amounts of fossil fuels. Chemical fertilizers, used to grow the feed crops for cattle in feedlots and pigs and chickens kept indoors in sheds, produce nitrous oxide, another greenhouse gas. Then there is the loss of forests. Everywhere, forest-dwellers, both human and non-human, can be pushed out." Peter Singer, **Practical Ethics**

Since 1960, 25 percent of the forests of Central America have been cleared for cattle. Once cleared, the poor soils will support grazing for a few years; then the grazers must move on. Shrubs take over the abandoned pasture, but the forest does not return. When the forests are cleared so the cattle can graze, billions of tons of carbon dioxide are released into the atmosphere.

Finally, the world's cattle are thought to produce about 20 percent of the methane released into the atmosphere, and methane traps twenty-five times as much heat from the sun as carbon dioxide. Factory farm manure also produces methane because, unlike manure dropped naturally in the fields, it does not decompose in the presence of oxygen. All of this amounts to a compelling reason for a plant-based diet.

Harsh facts about raising beef cows for food: it takes 12 pounds of grain to add one pound of meat on a cow. It takes 2,500 gallons of water to add one pound of beef on a bovine. The average mature dairy cow, which weighs about 900 lbs., produces about 82 pounds of raw manure each day that equals 29,000 pounds annually. Source: Texas State Energy Conservation Office's report. The average cow drinks and excretes up to 50 gallons of water daily. (22) (Source: www.earthsave.org)

One and a half billion cows eat, crap, expel methane gas and more 24/7. Enormous amounts of fossil fuels are burned to feed them, transport them, milk them, slaughter them and take them to market. Once we reach 439 million hungry people, will we possess enough water, energy and arable land to continue this enterprise?

With 1.5 billion cows on the globe, planet Earth must deal with trillions of pounds/gallons of manure waste, water waste and carbon footprint waste to feed the animals. Combined with the amount of fuel, arable land and water to grow the corn and grain encompassed in filling the stomachs of beef cows, "Houston, we've got a problem."

By growing our population to the projected 439 million by 2050, America faces sobering realities not being considered.

"A United Nations report has identified the world's rapidly growing herds of cattle as the greatest threat to the climate, forests and wildlife," said Geoffrey Lean, environmental editor of The Independent. "And they are blamed for a host of other environmental crimes, from acid rain to the introduction of alien species, from producing deserts to creating dead zones in the oceans, from poisoning rivers and drinking water to destroying coral reefs."

The 400 page report by the Food and Agricultural Organization, entitled "Livestock's Long Shadow," also surveys the damage done by sheep, chickens, pigs and goats. But in almost every case, the world's 1.5 billion cattle are most to blame. Livestock are responsible for 18 per cent of the greenhouse gases that cause global climate change, more than cars, planes and all other forms of transport put together.

Bovine overgrazing worldwide constitutes the major driver for deforestation. Eventually, those pastures turn to deserts. One liter (just over a quart) of milk requires 990 liters of water to produce it. That equates to 989-liters of waste-water the planet must tolerate. (Source: www. cowspiracy.com)

Steaming and toxic billions of tons of cow manure cannot be handled by the Natural World. It poisons the soil, groundwater and atmosphere. Over 1.5 billion cows create inexhaustible waste worldwide in our water, oceans, land and air.

Feedlots and fertilizers over-nourish water, causing weeds to choke all other life. The vast array of pesticides, antibiotics and hormones ultimately migrate into drinking water and endanger human health. In dairy farm states like Wisconsin, Illinois, Michigan and Ohio—ground water contamination creates mega-poisoning for humans and animals alike. Cancer: Sandra Steingraber wrote a book about cancer caused by contaminated ground water, rivers and lagoons—**Living Down Stream.**

Agricultural contamination washes down to the sea, killing coral reefs, and creates "dead zones" devoid of vertebrate life forms. The Mississippi River absorbs and transports mega-trillions of gallons of contaminated water into the Gulf of Mexico. Recent reports show a 10,000 square mile dead zone in New Orleans. Caution: eat shrimp at your own risk.

The mind-numbing damage can only grow by insane degrees as the human race adds another 2.2 billion of itself by 2050.

"Our choices as consumers drive an industry that kills ten billion animals per year in the United States alone. If we choose to support this industry and the best reason we can come up with is because it's the way things are, clearly something is amiss. What could cause an entire society of people to check their thinking caps at the door—and to not even realize they're doing so? Though this question is quite complex, the answer is quite simple: carnism." Melanie Joy, **Why We Love Dogs, Eat Pigs, and Wear Cows: An Introduction to Carnism: The Belief System That Enables Us to Eat Some Animals and Not Others.**

CHAPTER 16

//

FUKUSHIMA OVERFLOW

"Humankind has not woven the web of life. We are but one thread within it. Whatever we do to the web, we do to ourselves. All things are bound together. All things connect." Chief Seattle

Fukushima radioactive effluent circulating into all oceans

Twenty-nine months after Fukushima's nuclear power plants exploded, March 11, 2011, and started leaking millions-billions of gallons of radioactive toxic waste into the Pacific Ocean, the contaminated liquid circulated into all of the oceans around the world.

Fact: that radioactive waste enters into every living creature in the Earth's oceans and contaminates their flesh. If you eat salmon, tuna, shrimp and other marine creatures in 2021, you cannot help but absorb, to some degree, the radioactive contamination of Fukushima.

That single catastrophe may spell greater disasters for humans and all living creatures in the seas around the planet—for decades to come. As one writer said, "We're all standing on the beach for this one."

"Radiation readings around tanks holding contaminated water at the crippled Fukushima nuclear plant have spiked by more than a fifth to their highest levels," said Japan's nuclear regulator Alan Sheldrik, Tokyo. "It heightens concerns about the clean-up of the worst atomic disaster in almost three decades.

The NRA later raised the severity of the initial leak from a level 1 "anomaly" to a level 3 "serious incident" on an international scale of 1-7 for radiation releases.

"There's a strong possibility these tanks also leaked, or had leaked previously," said Hiroaki Koide, Assistant Professor at Kyoto University Research Reactor Institute. "We have to worry about the impact on nearby groundwater...These tanks are not sturdy and have been a problem since they were constructed two years ago."

The Plague of Plastics All Made from Oil

Along with Fukushima, plastics and chemicals overflow in rivers around the world, yet humans continue polluting them at breakneck speeds. Few if any pick up the plastic trash or containers in developing countries. They walk through it, avoid it, drink the water, but never think to take responsibility to pick it up or stop it.

What bothers me as a food consuming, water drinking and air breathing human being on this planet stems from the reality that we humans continue our mass contamination of our planet at rapacious speed.

If you look at the swirling radioactive plumes flying out of Japan on every ocean current—you see that Fukushima's radioactive waters spread to every nook and cranny of every ocean in the world.

The Taj Mahal, India looks so beautiful in the distance and we admire its beauty around the world. Near it, a plastic-filled river desecrates the land. Look what India does to its Natural World as it discards trillions of pieces of plastic into the Indian Ocean. What sinks to the bottom of the oceans causes death and destruction to eco-systems. Why haven't the world leaders come together to form a 50-cent deposit/return law for all plastic, glass and metal containers to ensure such pollution stops? Answer: they don't care and neither do the people of the world.

As to Fukushima, when the entire story comes to light and countless thousands and even millions of humans suffer from radiation poisoning, cancers and heaven knows what else—we must ask ourselves how much further we humans want to ride this planet down into a hell-hole of consequences.

We spray billions of tons of pesticides and insecticides onto our plants 24/7 here in the USA and abroad. Ironically, we outlawed DDT in the USA in the 1960's because of Rachel Carson's book: **Silent Spring.** But Chevron Company still makes it and sells it to people around the world. I know because I smelled it in my bicycle travels in Asia and South America. We know it kills all life and destroys ecological systems, but for the love of money, Chevron keeps selling that DDT lethal crap abroad. Unfortunately, like the Fukushima disaster, 84,000 chemical poisons that we created also spread around the world 24/7.

Consequently, cancers affect one in three people here in the United States and cancers grow worldwide as we continue our quest to soak the planet with chemicals. Cancer escalates as the number one cause of death in the world. The more we continue our plundering and polluting of this miraculous globe, the more we shall face Mother Nature's wrath in various forms: tornadoes caused in January in Illinois or massive killer tornadoes in Oklahoma that kill and destroy anyone in their paths. Those occur because of our massive carbon footprint unbalancing of Earth's weather patterns.

We acidify the oceans that continue their death spiral with radioactive wastes from Fukushima. Not known by most Americans, we dumped billions of pounds of mustard gas, Sarin and Lucite gas into the oceans after WWII. We dumped over 47,800 barrels of radioactive waste 20 miles off San Francisco, California in the 1950's. Today, all those drums rusted open and spewed their contents into the Pacific waters. We continue to draw down aquifers and contaminate ground water at the same time in the USA with massive pig farms, cattle farms and industrial waste.

(Source: Herman Karl, between 1946 and 1970, approximately 47,800 large containers of low-level radioactive waste were dumped in the Pacific Ocean west of San Francisco. These containers, mostly 55-gallon drums, were to be dumped at three designated sites in the Gulf of the Farallones.)

The drums actually litter a 540 square miles area of sea floor, much of it in what is now the Gulf of the Farallones National Marine Sanctuary, which was established by Congress in 1981.

(Source: https://pubs.usgs.gov/circ/c1198/chapters/207-217_RadWaste.pdf)

Most Americans do not possess a clue as to the global water crisis, but it is coming to America faster as our population increases.

If you could see what I saw as to raw sewage-chemicals injected into the Yangtze River in China, Ganges River in India, Rimac River in Peru, Hudson, Mississippi and Potomac Rivers in the USA, and many other rivers in South America—it would cause you to mentally vomit.

At some point, we human beings, whether Americans or planetary citizens from other countries must take stock of what we are doing to the planet and doing to ourselves.

If we keep going in the same direction we tread today, the 21st century will prove a bumpy ride for all of humanity along with all the other creatures in our path.

CHAPTER 17

//

EXPANDING GREENHOUSE GASES

"A simple look at the upward path of global greenhouse emissions indicates we will continue to squeeze the trigger on the gun we have put to our own head." Eugene Linden, The Winds of Change: Climate, Weather and the Destruction of Civilization

Worldwide, millions upon millions of smokestacks exhaust billions of tons of chemicals, carbon dioxide and particulate into the air 24/7. Those chemicals fall as acid rain on the land and into oceans. They change the chemistry of the soil, water and oceans. All of it deadly.

In the United States, 274,000,000 vehicles (23), and millions of planes, boats, trains, lawn mowers, snow machines and other combustion engines burn fuel 24/7. They exhaust enormous amounts of pollution every second without end.

In the United States, millions of homes, office buildings, schools and factories burn billions of tons of energy to operate the engines of commerce. They also exhaust billions of tons of carbon pollution.

It all adds up to an enormous load on the Natural World that cannot be mitigated.

At some point, something must give, and it will! Systems that cannot withstand the assault cannot help but collapse.

Mother Nature Deforms to Fit Humanity's Onslaught

Earth's average temperature rose 1.4 degrees Fahrenheit over the past century. Scientists project a rise of 2.0 degrees F to 11.0 degrees F within this century.

Small changes in the average temperature of the planet translate to large and dangerous shifts in climate and weather. It also transforms our oceans given temperature changes and acidification from carbon infusing into the water.

Previous to the Industrial Revolution, the Earth's atmosphere carried 280 parts per million (average for millennia) of carbon dioxide. On January 26, 2017, that figure rose to over 400 ppm for the first time in millions of years. (24)

Since that time, oil, gas and coal became energy sources that overwhelm the Natural World's ability to mitigate their impact.

The evidence grows stronger with each passing year. Rising global temperatures caused greater magnitude of Hurricane Katrina, Sandy and Haiyan in the Philippines. Tornadoes touch down in February throughout the Midwest in America.

Many regions face extreme drought like California while extremes express themselves all over the planet. Glaciers melt with increasing speed in Asia, Greenland, Antarctica and Alaska.

From personal experience, I spent six months in Antarctica to see glaciers calve from the continent. Some were bigger than the State of Rhode Island. We're talking monster-sized icebergs.

Additionally, I've watched glaciers severely retreat in Alaska and British Columbia over the past 40 years when I cycled to the Arctic Circle.

The Driving Carbon Energy of Overpopulation

Cities around the world house up to 37 million residents, such as Tokyo, Japan, that intensify air pollution and carbon footprint. Delhi, India features 29 million. Shanghai boasts 26 million. Mexico City groans from 20 million. Lung cancer rates rise while water pollution rates scream off the charts. Everyone breathes toxic air with every breath 24/7.

Oceans warm while becoming more acidic, which translates into unlivable habitat for marine creatures. Extinction follows.

So, what's causing our massive environmental warming trend?

Essentially, Human Beings Are Burning Up the Planet

The United Nations weather agency chief Michel Jarraud said, "Ocean temperatures are rising fast, and extreme weather events, forecast by climate scientists, showed climate change was inevitable for the coming centuries. There is no standstill in global warming. The year 2019 tied with 2007 as the sixth hottest year since 1850 when recording of annual figures began. The year 2020 topped the charts!"

New Heat Records Annually

"The warming of our oceans has accelerated, and at lower depths," Jarraud said. "More than 90 percent of the excess energy trapped by greenhouse gases is stored in the oceans. Levels of these greenhouse gases are at a record, meaning that our atmosphere and oceans will continue to warm for centuries to come. The laws of physics are non-negotiable."

We humans set a course beyond our understanding. We tinker with the mechanism of climate and ecology beyond our capacity. We very well could become our own executioner along with many of our fellow travelers.

Shallow-water creatures, like corals, are extremely vulnerable to carbonic acid. Scientists are calling for drastic measures to avert massive bleaching of the world's reefs.

Scientists understand the Earth's oceans absorbed half of anthropogenic, or man-made CO_2 since 1850. But research shows that introduction of massive amounts of CO_2 into the seas alters water chemistry, which affects the life cycles of many marine organisms throughout the food chain.

Carbonic Acid: When carbon dioxide dissolves in the ocean, carbonic acid forms. This leads to higher acidity, which inhibits shell growth in marine animals and causes reproductive disorders in some fish. On the "pH" scale, which runs from 0 to 14, solutions with low numbers are considered acidic and those with higher numbers are basic. Seven is neutral. Over the past 300 million years, ocean "pH" measured "basic", averaging 8.2. Today, it is around 8.1, a drop of 0.1 "pH" units, representing a 25 percent increase in acidity over the past two centuries.

During an overpopulation conference in Washington DC, I attended a lecture by Dr. Camilo Mora, Professor of Geography at the University of Hawaii. He said, "When you look at the world's oceans, there are few places that will be free of changes; most will suffer the simultaneous effects of warming, acidification, and reductions in oxygen and productivity.

"The consequences of these co-occurring changes are massive—everything from species survival, to abundance, to range size, to body size, to species richness, to ecosystem functioning are affected by changes in ocean biogeochemistry."

Humpback whales are among the many whales that feed on krill, which will be subject to multiple climate stressors.

If we humans continue our 24/7 carbon footprint attack on Mother Nature, she will respond without mercy. For example: if the oceans become overly acidic, the krill that feeds endless numbers of creatures in our oceans may go extinct. If they die, the entire food chain dies.

It's called "cascading extinctions." As one creature in the chain dies off, everything that fed upon that creature dies off in a chain-reaction that cascades into massive extinction rates for other dependent creatures.

After reading the aforementioned facts, what do you think we face?

Should we accept our fate and keep heading down the same road? Is that what you want for your kids?

If you would like to see what kind of a healthy planet we inherited in the past 100 years, please watch David Attenborough's documentary series on Netflix. He covers what a beautiful planet we've enjoyed up until about the last 100 years.

"Blue Planet" shows the utter perfection of the Natural World around this globe.

"Frozen Planet" shows the sheer beauty of the Arctic, Antarctic and winter scenarios.

"Light on Earth" shows incredible beauty on Earth.

"A Plastic Ocean" shows the devastating destruction of our oceans from our outrageous tossing of 5.25 trillion pieces of plastic into them over the past 56 years.

"Life on This Planet" depicts the destruction we have wrought upon this planet in the 20th and 21st centuries.

CHAPTER 18

///

THIS HEART WITHIN ME BURNS

"The world is reaching the tipping point beyond which climate change may become irreversible. If this happens, we risk denying present and future generations the right to a healthy and sustainable planet – the whole of humanity stands to lose." Kofi Annan, Former Secretary-General of UN

Bird Life on Midway Island in the Pacific Ocean and the Onslaught of Plastics

Samuel Taylor Coleridge wrote, "Until my ghastly tale is told; this heart within me burns." From his epic work: **The Rime of the Ancient Mariner.**

This ghastly, if not poignant look onto Midway Island, 2,000 miles out in the Pacific Ocean, reminds us of the sublime beauty of our planet via the Waved Albatross, but at the same time, how fast humanity's plastics ravage the natural world. The following four-minute video allows you a mind-changing look into humanity's assault on the Natural World. It depicts seabirds choking on plastic bottle caps they ingest and dying by the hundreds of thousands because the plastic pieces clog their guts.

"This Awful Thing We Do" available on YouTube.

http://www.upworthy.com/people-should-know-about-this-awful-thing-we-do-and-most-of-us-are-simply-unaware?c=ufb1

Hopefully, the four minutes you took to watch this sobering—if not stomach-churning video—gives you the courage to speak up, take action and push for 50 cent deposit-return laws on every piece of plastic that leaves our stores across America and around the planet.

You must take action with your state and federal leaders to stop further damage to our Natural World. Our civilization and all civilizations around the globe must implement 50-cent plastic-deposit-return laws if we hope to salvage what's left of the health of our oceans worldwide. We need to implement effective educational systems in order to make every world citizen responsible for that plastic bottle cap, toothbrush holder, soft drink container, Styrofoam cooler and another 100,000 plastic items that we buy and toss 24/7 around the planet.

Animal life cannot distinguish between nutrient foods and plastic. You've seen pictures of beached whales with enough plastic of every description in their bellies to force their painful and slow deaths by choking and starvation. Despite this ongoing atrocity, humans refuse to engage plastic-deposit-return laws or change containers to glass in 2021, and heaven only knows how far into the future. We should not manufacture plastic bottle caps or anything that can fall into the mouths of the creatures of the Natural World.

Global leaders and manufacturing CEO's echo similar disregard for our Natural World. Poisons abound because of Dow Chemical, Monsanto, Bayer and Chevron. As to average citizens around the world, they remain clueless as to their discard of plastics.

Countless millions of seabirds suffer the fate of the ones you saw in the video with plastic-loaded bellies that they had mistaken for food. If world leaders and manufacturing CEO's possessed an ounce of morality-ethics-personal accountability over the money, they make—this horrendous "ghastly tale" could be solved.

When Coca Cola hit 100 years of age, the CEO boasted, "I am so proud to bring Coke to the world."

In reality, via my world travels, I watched countless kids and parents smiling with toothless mouths because they suffered caffeine-sugar addiction from Coke and other soft drinks. They lack any access to toothbrushes and floss. Today, we know that soft drinks create heart problems and obesity. Would the CEO of Coke take action to stop his drink from circulating around the world to render millions of toothless smiles? Would he add a toothbrush and floss to every purchase of his product? Would he support deposit-return laws for his plastic containers? Answer: what do you think?

Marine life worldwide strangles itself on plastic debris circulating around the planet on the surface and beneath the waves. Humans kill 100 million sharks annually (that figure is correct and has gone on annually for over 30 years) and heaven only knows how many die from ingesting plastics before they die, sinking to the bottom where there is no way to count their numbers.

In Daniel Quinn's book, **Ishmael**, he said, **"And yet you do destroy the planet, each of you. Each of you contributes daily to the destruction of the world. You're captives of a civilizational system that more or less compels you to go on destroying the world in order to live."**

Every island beach around the world features plastics that float up to land on the sand. Trillions of pieces of plastic of every description continue their onslaught on wildlife and the Natural World. What do humans do? In the last 55 years since they invented plastics, humans continue tossing it into the oceans with no pause in sight.

As you saw from the four-minute video, we witness and understand the damage, but we fail to take action.

If we live out Eleanor Roosevelt's quote to its "ghastly finish" and fail to take action—we face acidified oceans where marine life cannot live and procreate. We suffer obliteration of plankton that create 80 percent of the oxygen we breathe on this planet. We face warming oceans via carbon footprint from fossil fuel burning, which in turn, destroys our climatic systems worldwide.

All marine life continues to eat and incorporate those mini-particles of plastic into their systems, until, when we eat them, we pay the same consequences you saw from the albatross on Midway Island. (Source: At least half of Earth's oxygen comes from the ocean. The surface layer of the ocean is teeming with photosynthetic plankton. Scientists estimate that 50 to 80 percent of the oxygen production on Earth comes from the ocean. www.oceanservice.noaa.gov)

Frankly, are you optimistic that humans share the collective will or acumen to save themselves? Do we possess any chance to turn this nightmare around? Will we move on information found in this video and these pictures to change the way we use plastics around the world?

Because the United States citizens use 2.0 million, that's 2,000,000 plastic bottles every five minutes and discard them—we need to take action darned fast.

Very few people comprehend the enormity of the plastics onslaught around our planet. Again, it's floating and landing not only on beaches, but under the oceans as well. In its wake, utter devastation on eco-systems, marine life and, in the end a "ghastly tale" for all of humanity.

CHAPTER 19

//

THE GARBAGE-WASTE CONUNDRUM

"American cities are like badger holes, ringed with trash—all of them—surrounded by piles of wrecked and rusting automobiles, and smothered with rubbish. Everything we use comes in boxes, cartons, bins, the so-called packaging we love so much. The mountains of things we throw away are much greater than the things we use. In this, if no other way, we can see the wild and reckless exuberance of our production, and waste seems to be the index. I wonder whether there will come a time when we can no longer afford our wastefulness—chemical wastes in the rivers, metal wastes everywhere, and atomic wastes buried deep in the earth or sunk in the sea. When an Indian village became too deep in its own filth, the inhabitants moved. And we have no place to move." — John Steinbeck, Travels with Charley: In Search of America

Garbage, Waste, Refuse in America and Worldwide.

In 2021, the United States generates 4.4 pounds of trash per person 24/7. (Source: www.EnvironmentalProtectionAgency.gov, According to the EPA, the average American person will produce about 5.91 pounds of trash, with about 1.51 pounds being recycled; 4.40 pounds is the average daily waste per person.)

Americans throw 251 million tons of trash annually into landfills, lakes, rivers and oceans.

We throw more trash than most of the rest of the world, but they catch up annually as they grow their populations by 83 million each year. China expects to use and toss over 900 to 1,200 million tires annually as they continue their quest to be more like Americans. The U.S. discards 250 million tires annually.

Plastic bags: 60,000—Number of plastic bags consumed in the U.S. every 5 seconds. Number of plastic bags consumed worldwide every 10 seconds—240,000. (Source: Sierra Club, "Plastic trash.)

1 billion—Number of plastic bags Americans use every year. (Source: Clean Air Council)

30,000 tons—Landfill waste created from plastic bags each year.

Less than 1 percent—Amount of plastic bags that are recycled.

The amount of garbage we discard numbs a thinking person's mind and stupefies anyone who thinks about the ramifications of our future.

Paper

15 million—Sheets of office paper used in the U.S. every 5 minutes. The average American uses roughly the equivalent of one 100-foot-tall Douglas fir tree in paper and wood products each year. (Source: www. EnvironmentalProtectionAgency.gov)

100 million—Number of trees cut down in the U.S. annually to make the paper for junk mail.

9,960—Pieces of junk mail that are printed, shipped, delivered and disposed of in the U.S. every three seconds.

2.4 million pounds—Amount of plastic pollution that enters the world's oceans every hour.

1 million—Number of plastic cups that are consumed on airline flights in the U.S. every six hours.

2 million—Number of plastic beverage bottles that are used in the U.S. every five minutes. The number of plastic water bottles discarded in the U.S. every week could circle the Earth five times.

The more I dove into the research for this book, the more I felt sickened at what I discovered. When you pile up the numbers for the USA, it's overwhelming. When you pile up the numbers for India, China and other overpopulated countries, it's downright staggering. We add 1.0 billion humans every 12 years—so the trash numbers will continue to climb. Our oceans will continue to be degraded. But no one will address it; not one single world leader. (Source: www.pbs.org, "We're adding a billion population every 12 years.")

E-waste

20 to 50 million metric tons—Amount of electronics the world throws away annually. That's the equivalent of trashing 45,500 to 125,000 fully loaded 747's each year. (Source: www.Ewasteguide.info)

10 to 18 percent—Amount of electronics that are recycled.

304 million—Electronics disposed of from U.S. households in 2005 — two-thirds of them still worked.

18,500—Number of homes that could be powered for a year if we recycled all of the cellphones retired annually.

All totaled, the USA discards 251 million tons of trash annually. How do you compare that number? (Source: www.Environmental ProtectionAgency.gov)

The United States discards more than 4,837 Titanic's filled with trash in a normal calendar year. If that blows your mental circuits, think about how much the rest of the world discards in trash.

Unfortunately, it drips, drains, funnels and wafts into the land, air and water. We face "payback" in the coming years on a scale unheard of in human history.

Worldwide, humans produce 1.2 kg per person per day or 1.3 billion tons per year. By 2025 this will increase to 4.3 billion urban residents generating about 1.42 kg/capita/day of municipal solid waste, 2.2 million tons per year.

Finally, Americans waste or cause to be wasted nearly one million pounds of materials per person every year. This figure includes 3.5 billion pounds of carpet landfilled, 3.3 trillion pounds of CO_2 gas emitted into the atmosphere, 19 billion pounds of polystyrene peanuts, 28 billion pounds of food discarded, 360 billion pounds of organic and inorganic chemicals used for manufacturing, 710 billion pounds of hazardous waste and 3.7 trillion pounds of construction debris.

- If wastewater is factored in, the total annual flow of waste in the American Industrial System equals 250 trillion pounds.
- Less than 2.0 percent of the total waste stream in the United States enjoys recycling.
- For all the world to live as an American, we would need two more Earths; three more if the population should double and twelve Earth's altogether if worldwide standards of living doubled in the next forty years.

Our trash reaches the Arctic Ocean where polar bears, whales, seagulls and seals must contend with our accelerating nightmare. Trash does the same damage in the Southern Oceans of Antarctica.

Somewhere down the line, Mother Nature will kick our rear-ends back to the Stone Age.

CHAPTER 20

//

FISHING EARTH'S OCEANS TO DEATH

"The oceans of today are filled with ghost habitats, stripped of their larger inhabitants. Our dismantling of marine ecosystems is having destructive and unpredictable consequences. With species loss and food-web collapse comes dangerous instability. The seas are undergoing ecological meltdown. Fishing is undermining itself by purging the oceans of species on which it depends. The wholesale removal of marine life and obliteration of their habitats is stripping resilience from ocean ecosystems." Oceanographer Callum Roberts

Fishing Our Oceans to Death; Surface of a Haunted Ocean

At 95 million tons of fish netted annually, the oceans cannot withstand humanity's onslaught. At some point, like the extinct Carrier Pigeon, untold species of marine life face extinction. (26)

The Natural World staggers back on its heels.

Fully 80 percent of all life on this planet thrives beneath the surface of our oceans. This enormous body of water pulses with life-energy, which drives natural forces that sustain all living creatures on this planet. But in the 21st century the "Human Mob" wreaks havoc on the foundation of life on Earth. It hooks, pollutes, skims, nets and daggers untold billions of creatures to death annually.

While Roberts brings his powerful research to the table, most of humankind remains oblivious to catastrophic onslaught raging beneath the waves. As a 58 year scuba diver, I watched it progress from the Gulf of Mexico into all of our oceans.

With America's 330 million people devouring ocean marine life such as squid, crabs, shrimp, tuna, salmon, flounder, swordfish, whales, dolphins and so many other species—take a look at what 7.8 billion humans devour worldwide:

Giant ships, using state-of-the-art equipment throw out 1.5-mile-long drift nets that capture **95 million tons** of marine life annually. These industrial fishing fleets exceed the ocean's ecological limits. As larger fish dwindle in numbers, the next smaller fish species are targeted and so on. A Canadian fisheries expert Dr. Daniel Pauly warns that if this continues, "Our children will be eating jellyfish."

Factory fishing ships with 1.5-mile-long drift nets encircle hapless marine life, killing countless creatures as "bycatch" while they scoop up endless fish for consumption by 7.8 billion humans.

For the past 30 years, humans continue their annihilation of all species of sharks by killing them at a rate of 100 million sharks annually. You must wonder, "How much longer can this kind of a killing spree continue before the sharks and all ocean life reach a point of no return?" (Source: "Predator Becomes the Prey" ; Life Magazine August 1991; Julia Whitty, **Onearth Magazine**)

The latest threat grows beyond solving with "carbon footprint" waste from fossil fuel burning at 99 million barrels of oil daily and billions of tons of coal and natural gas annually—to overload our seas with carbon that acidifies the oceans to a point whereby marine life can no longer exist in the toxic ocean water. It would be like you taking a bath in carbonic acid water.

Another aspect of humanity's "deadly treatment" of our oceans deals with the phenomenon of "dead zones" at the mouths of all our major rivers worldwide. For instance, the Ganges and Yangtze rivers exhaust their toxic sewage waters into the world's oceans 24/7 to create 20,000 square mile dead zones. The water grows so lethal that higher forms of marine life cannot exist in those zones. In America, the Mississippi River spews chemical waste, petroleum waste and endless sewage waste to create a 10,000 square mile dead zone at its mouth in New Orleans.

WWII major war powers dumped their mustard gas, oil and other chemicals along with radioactive waste into the oceans of the world.

Humanity's 84,000 chemicals always end up in the oceans as their final toilet destination.

Over time, those toxic rivers exhausting out of Europe, Asia, South America, Russia and North America cannot help but chemically contaminate the oceans of the world. That means all the fish in them consume the chemicals they breathe and eat in their daily existence. With the latest Fukushima radioactive waste spill of trillions of gallons of toxic liquids, our oceans cannot help but stagger to keep their "pH" balance. Fukushima spreading:

http://www.conspiracy-watch.org/fukushima-radiation-is-in-america/

When you include the 100 million ton, the size of Texas, (and growing by 8.0 million plastic pieces per day), "The Great Pacific Garbage Patch", which constitutes a floating plastic island and hangs 1,000 miles off San Francisco—you cannot help but understand that we humans desecrate our nest at blinding speed. Soberingly, researchers tell us that 46,000 pieces of plastic float on every square mile of our oceans. Those constitute sickening statistics.

Is it little wonder that marine life cannot survive the plastic onslaught of their environment? Ocean beaches around the world feature this plastic filth. I regret to report that I've stood in knee deep plastic on some beaches.

Plastic killing zone at Midway Island:

http://www.upworthy.com/people-should-know-about-this-awful-thing-we-do-and-most-of-us-are-simply-unaware?c=ufb1

Do the oceans stand a chance when we remain on course to add another three billion of our species within 29 years? Answer: not a snowball's chance in hell!

So, when you read a sobering book like this that reports on the underpinnings of humanity's dilemma, what do you think? What do you do? How do you do it? When do you start?

It's my contention that environmental leaders and demographic experts rattle the bars, scream at the media and make noise in every country around the world. Silence won't cut it fellow humans. We need 7.8 billion

Greta Thunberg's and Adam Roberti's in this world. Mr. Roberti, after having graduated from the University of Miami, teaches at the Cortada Science Art Academy in Pinecrest Gardens, Florida to educate and inspire youth to take action on the environment.

The Cortada Science Art Academy at Pinecrest Gardens teaches students how to think, imagine, and problem-solve while caring for the environment. Developed by Xavier Cortada, renowned eco-artist and Pinecrest Gardens' Artist-in-Residence, this immersive, outdoor after-school program develops engaged citizens who use art and science to better understand our world, connect with others, and address environmental concerns.

Students dive deep into Cortada's science art practice to discover how they can use the power of art to spur social and environmental action. Through engaged studio sessions and presentations at Pinecrest Gardens' Hammock Pavilion, students learn how to use creativity and leadership to help conserve Florida's ecosystems, defend global biodiversity, and advance the work of climate scientists at the Earth's poles.

To learn more about the Cortada Science Art Academy, visit www.cortadaacademy.org, info@cortadaacademy.org, or follow on social media @cortadaacademy.

In other words, all of us must become active. You need to engage your courage, your guts, your true grit and your creative energy to move the discussion to the highest levels in the USA, Canada, Europe, Australia and beyond. If the Western world doesn't address this, no one else will touch it!

Finally, your kids won't be eating jellyfish; they will choke on seaweed.

Postscript:

Exactly 10 years before, when Newcastle yachtsman Ivan Macfadyen sailed the same course from Melbourne to Osaka, all he did to catch a fish from the ocean between Brisbane and Japan was throw out a baited line. (Source: October 21, 2013, www.theguardian.com)

"There was not one of the 28 days on that portion of the trip when we didn't catch a good-sized fish to cook up and eat with some rice," Macfadyen recalled.

But this time, on that whole long leg of sea journey, the total catch was two. No fish. No birds. Hardly a sign of life at all.

"In years gone by, I'd gotten used to all the birds and their noises," he said.

"They'd be following the boat, sometimes resting on the mast before taking off again. You'd see flocks of them wheeling over the surface of the sea in the distance, feeding on pilchards."

But in 2013, only silence and desolation surrounded his boat, *Funnel Web*, as it sped across the surface of a haunted ocean.

"Moreover, it is undermining the ability of the oceans to support human needs. Overfishing is destabilizing the marine environment, contributing to the spread of anoxic dead zones and the increasing prevalence of toxic algal blooms. Nature's power to bounce back after catastrophes or absorb the battery of stresses humanity is subjecting it to is being eroded, collapsed fishery after collapsed fishery, species by species, place by place." —**Callum Roberts, The Unnatural History of the Sea**

CHAPTER 21

///

GENETICALLY MODIFIED ORGANISMS: UNLEASHING 21ST CENTURY FRANKENSTEIN ON THE NATURAL WORLD

"Cows given genetically modified growth hormones make more milk, but have painful swollen udders, have ulcers, joint pain, miscarriages, deformed calves, infertility, and much shorter life spans. Their milk contains blood, pus, tranquilizers, antibiotics, and an insulin growth factor that can cause a fourfold increase in prostate cancer and sevenfold rise in breast cancer. This is the milk used in our school lunch programs and served to our children. This is the milk used in all cheeses, yogurts, butter, and cream." Kevin Trudeau, More Natural Cures Revealed

Changing the DNA Structure of Mother Nature

In the 20st century, the human mob re-arranged rivers, deserts, rainforests and the oceans to suit its voracious appetite for dominance over the Natural World. Stemming from that 100 year onslaught, we humans created communities around the globe featuring 10 million, 20 million to 36 million people piled into mega-cities around the planet.

We contaminated rivers with our poisons, the air with our fossil fuel exhaust and clear-cut rainforests by the millions of acres. Our onslaught of the Natural World continues with 100 species of our fellow travelers losing their existence 24/7 to our encroachment upon their habitat. (Source: Norman Myers, Oxford University)

One of our most destructive acts continues on the bees and other pollinators around the world. In the past 50 years, we poisoned every crop with hundreds of chemical herbicides, pesticides and chemical fertilizers, which, in turn, caused trillions of bees to suffer "Colony Collapse" throughout the world. Without the bees, which I wrote about earlier, our species cannot feed itself.

To add insult to injury in the 21st century, in order to feed our 7.8 billion in numbers, we began tinkering with the structural DNA of plants and animals.

Changing the DNA of Our Crops by Monsanto via GMO Foods

"Genetically modified foods may look and feel the same as conventional foods, but they are drastically different. These types of foods have been altered by taking the genetic material (DNA) from one species and transferring it into another in order to obtain a desired trait. The FDA does not require any safety testing or any labeling of GMO foods, and introducing new genes into a fruit or vegetable may very well be creating unknown results such as new toxins, new bacteria, new allergens, and new diseases." M.D. David Brownstein, **The Guide to Healthy Eating**

Today, our scientists change the DNA patterns of fish and plants in order to make them bigger, grow faster and yield more harvest: genetically modified organisms.

But we forgot to ask Mother Nature if our meddling in her business would cause any harm. Amazingly, we allow governments, scientists on the payroll of companies like ADM and Monsanto, to tell us that such activities work to make our lives better with no harm to the natural world.

With my research on GMO's connecting their horrific harm to the Natural World and ultimately to we humans, this book will show you the "GMO Frankenstein" being foisted upon us by unethical businessmen in high places who could care less about you, your family or the rest of the species sharing this planet with us.

My intention in writing this book: to educate you to the mind-boggling damage GMO foods cause you along with your family and more important: the horrific destruction to the Natural World.

Ultimately, humans tinker and destroy the DNA foundation of the Natural World. Monarch butterflies are on the verge of extinction, which will cause more extinctions of other insects.

If you look at human cancers spreading like wildfire across America along with the rest of the world, and every physical ailment we face in America, along with the accelerating damage to bees, other pollinators and to the fish in our oceans—you will become appalled at this onslaught and its final consequences.

"If manufacturers are so sure there is nothing wrong with genetically modified foods, pesticides and cloned meats, they should have no problems labeling them as such. After all, 'cancer will kill one in every two men and one in every three women now alive," reports Samuel Epstein, chairman of the Cancer Prevention Coalition. "The military-industrial complex lubricates the mass-agriculture system with fossil fuels. Tons of heavy metals and other hazardous, even radioactive waste is sprayed on American agricultural soil." Adam Leith Gollner, **The Fruit Hunters: A Story of Nature, Adventure, Commerce and Obsession**

Investigative reporter Jeremy Siefert said, "When people first hear about the basic facts concerning Genetically Modified Organisms, they gulp. The DNA of seeds altered with genes from other organisms are manufactured to withstand herbicides that will kill all other plants. They are patented by giant chemical companies and found in 80 percent of processed foods – the standard response is "Oh, my God."

For some, it's just an exclamation, but for others, it's the beginnings of a prayer, "Please God, what can I do to save my family from GMO's?" There's a mixture of horror and disbelief. You feel you've been duped. (Source: www.fairworldproject.org)

Even without understanding what a GMO is or why it matters, most of us believe as citizens of a *supposedly* free and democratic society that we have the right to know if GMO's are injected into the food we eat. The fact we don't know, and that our right to know has been taken away by corporate greed and government collusion, should upset and mobilize people. When all the food, seed, water and air are owned and patented by giant multinational corporations, will we protest? Do we have the wakefulness and willpower to take that first step and stand up for this basic right?

What I discovered in my research: ADM (Archer-Daniels-Midland Food Processing Company) and Monsanto **do not want you to know**, along with high government officials, the deleterious effects on the Natural World that GMO food production causes in the long run. These mega-giant corporations "own" regulatory agencies, government officials (bribes or dandy trips to Caribbean resorts), and other complicit chemical companies around the planet.

GMO corn destroys insect pollinators, confuses the Natural World and ultimately, subverts the DNA of our food chain.

Be warned: you will not like the kind of treachery being foisted upon you by your U.S. Congress and officials who should present a moral and ethical stance against GMO's, but fail us because of one item: money.

Thus, as we move through this book, you may choose to save yourself and your family by buying "Certified Organic Foods" along with "Certified Non-Genetically Modified Organism" foods that give you the nutrients of Mother Nature intended without the "Frankensteinization" of your food supply and of the planet's natural systems.

Additionally, Monsanto and other HUGE corporations work every angle to stop any "GMO" labeling of their poisonous foods. Why do you think they do that?

"We are eating hybridized and genetically modified foods full of antibiotics, hormones, pesticides, and additives that were unknown to our immune systems just a generation ago. The result? Our immune systems become unable to recognize friend or foe—to distinguish between foreign molecular invaders we truly need to protect against and the foods we eat, or in some cases our own cells." H.D. Hyman, MD

If this information educates you enough, you may take action provided in the organizations and leaders trying to rid the world of GMO's. Help them and ultimately, you will help your family.

Otherwise, if these "monsters" of Monsanto and ADM get their way, they will cripple this world, all living creatures and the structural systems that allow all life on Earth to remain in balance and allow us to thrive.

All of this food predicament stems from humanity's overpopulation of the world. It's about our species' overwhelming the carrying capacity of this planet. It's about the end result which will not be pretty for any living creature in the 21st century.

Reference books:

The GMO Deception: What you need to know about foods, corporations and government agencies putting our families at risk by Sheldon Krimski

Seeds of Deception: Exposing industry and government agencies about the safety of genetically engineered foods you eat by Jeffery Smith

Altered Genes, Twisted Truth: How the venture to genetically engineer our foods has subverted our science, corrupted governments and systematically deceived the public by Steven M. Druker

CHAPTER 22

///

HUMANITY'S 300 YEAR SELF-TERMINATING EXPERIMENT WITH INDUSTRIALISM

"Our persistent and ever-increasing extraction and utilization of NNR's (non-renewable natural resources)—the finite and non-replenishing fossil fuels, metals and nonmetallic minerals that enable our industrial existence—is causing increasingly pervasive global NNR scarcity, which is causing political instability, economic fragility, and societal unrest. This scenario will intensify during the coming decades and culminate in humanity's permanent global societal collapse, almost certainly by the year 2050." Christopher O. Clugston

Blip: Humanity's 300 Year Self-Terminating Experiment with Industrialism

America supports 330 million people who eat food, drive cars, consume everything in sight, and utilize over 80 different minerals and metals that make our civilization work. Those non-renewable natural resources allow us our extraordinarily mechanized, chemicalized and advanced society—as well as our extraordinary standard of living.

Today, 1.4 billion Chinese, 1.3 billion Indians and all total, 7.8 billion humans scour this planet for—ever decreasing amounts of non-renewable natural resources under the crust of this planet. Worse, within 29 years, 2.2 billion more humans will be added to rummage this planet for any remaining resources to keep the engines of commerce operating.

In 2021, humans eat food, consume water, burn fuels to keep warm, and essentially waste finite resources on a fixed planet. Soberingly, the more people we add, the faster we deplete those resources.

While everyone screams about "Catastrophic Climate Destabilization", few understand the "Exponential Growth Factor" that threatens our very existence as a viable species on this planet. Fewer still realize that "The Age of Oil" that makes our societies operate—will reach exhaustion by mid-century.

"What we do to enable our existence as an industrialized society simultaneously undermines our existence," said Christopher Clugston, author of the blockbuster book, **Blip.**

In other words, "This scenario will intensify during the coming decades and culminate in humanity's permanent global societal collapse, almost certainly by 2050." I personally spoke to Clugston before this book published. He said, "I may have been too optimistic about 2050. We face huge shortfalls by 2040."

I read Clugston's book. He articulates humanity's ever-increasing usage of resources that can never be duplicated within the context of "exponential human growth." What is exponential growth? It's the same as a cancer cell. It multiplies until it kills its host. Once NNR's suffer exhaustion, American society or any industrialized society cannot continue operating. Why? Because they lack the energy, metals, minerals and resources to continue.

Imagine a man who walks into the desert with two gallons of water, but given enough time in the desert, he runs out of water, however he's 50 miles from the nearest well. He sets out toward the well. The closer he walks to the well, the faster his own supply of water runs out. When he arrives at the well, he's out of water, but he finds the well has run dry, too. He's out of luck.

It's the classic Faustian Bargain, whereby he started out with ample water, so he wasted it, but he ends up with Hobson's Choice.

America, Canada, Australia and Europe may be riding high in 2021, but in 29 short years, Hobson's Choice cannot be avoided.

Clugston said, "Our impending collapse will result from our irreparably and irreversibly impaired global natural environment—specifically, from Earth's extensively depleted and/or decimated finite and non-replenishing, non-renewable natural resources—a circumstance that cannot be remedied."

Please note: no amount of "technology" will save us.

Restoration of our irreversibly depleted and irreparably impaired global natural environment will be physically impossible, as will restoration of human industrialism.

The bigger our cities around the globe, the faster and harder they will collapse as to water, energy, food and resources.

Clugston said, "While it is possible that some local and natural environments will remain favorable to support subsistence level agrarian societies comparable to those that existed prior to the inception of industrialism, the extraordinarily favorable, NNR-rich, global natural environment that enabled our 300 year industrial "blip" will be gone forever."

After reading Clugston's book, I am sobered as to the future of every single person living in Canada, America, Australia and Europe—and any big city country with millions of people to feed. Essentially, Clugston researched his book with the brilliance of an Einstein in the realm of resources.

As I sat in my seat researching the data, it dawned me that 330 million people need to eat 990 million meals every day of the week. That's three meals a day times 330 million people. When we hit 439 million people, it's difficult to wrap my mind around that many meals and what it takes to provide that much food on the dinner tables of all Americans.

If we fail to change course in this decade, we cast our fate to an inexorably bleak future. Along the way, we face more conflict over resources with China, India, Mexico, South America and across the planet.

Can we somehow mitigate our impending fate? Can we minimize the results? Can we give future generations a chance?

As a lay person in this arena, I propose a few solutions:

1. We MUST stop trashing our oceans with chemicals and plastics. We must force Monsanto-Bayer and Dow Chemical companies to quit screwing with our Natural World. Stop all poison productions. We must engage an international 50 cent deposit law on every piece of plastic, metal, and glass—to ensure its return for recycling.

2. We must define carrying capacity in every country and move toward sustainable societies.

3. As to America and Canada, huge consumers of resources, we MUST stop all immigration that is projected to add 100 million people to the USA by 2050 and over 10 million to Canada. It's simply not sustainable.

4. We must engage world leaders, environmentalists, biologists, population specialists, climate experts, ocean experts and, most of all, religious leaders to educate their followers as to the negative impacts of humans on this planet.

5. What solutions might you offer to this predicament?

Several colleagues asked me to talk about nuclear energy. It's an extraordinary source of power for big electrical plants, submarines and military ships. At the same time, it cannot easily be maneuvered into cars, busses and semi-trucks. Additionally, it's very dirty in that it releases radio-active waste that is lethal to all life, and that must find a disposal site. With a changing planet, that waste, at some point could leak into the groundwater, oceans and more. But in the end, the materials for nuclear power will also be exhausted, so we're back to square one. Please see the information regarding "waste burning" into alcohol for much cleaner energy. www.biorootenergy.org

Finally, do you think we humans will attempt to save ourselves? Will we make any effort to change course? As for me having observed humanity around the world for the past 50 years, it's a bit dicey as to which path we might choose. Will we continue toward the Faustian Bargain with a grand finale of Hobson's Choice? Or will we opt for what some call "The Darwinian Solution"? Or, maybe, just maybe, this book creates a much-needed discussion-debate across America and the world. What's your individual choice as well as action plan?

Read his book to see for yourself: **Blip: Humanity's 300 Year Self-Terminating Experiment with Industrialism** by Christopher Clugston, on Amazon, ISBN #978-1-64438-068-0

His other book: **Scarcity—Humanity's Final Chapter?** By Christopher Clugston, on Amazon.com, ISBN#978-1-62141-250-2

SECTION 3

ENVIRONMENTAL, SOCIOLOGICAL, QUALITY OF LIFE ISSUES

CHAPTER 23

///

IMMIGRATION RAMIFICATIONS

"Climate change is real. It is happening right now. It is the most urgent threat facing our entire species and we need to work collectively together and stop procrastinating."

Leonardo Di Caprio, Actor & Environmentalist

Every morning, noon and night, you hear the weather report forecasted in your specific area. Meteorologists warn you of approaching tornados, rainsqualls or blizzards. They warn you of breezes or high winds. You know the temperatures in order to dress correctly or not to drive that day.

Because of those forecasts, you make daily choices with knowledge and understanding. You protect yourself and your family.

Do you ever notice the evening news with 20 car pile-up crashes because humans drove into a blinding snowstorm? What about a cluster of 18 wheelers that drove into a fog bank only to create multiple deaths? As you look at the traffic standing still in your city, why did all those people drive their cars into such a gridlocked mess?

As you sit watching the evening news, you wonder, "Why did so many people make such stupid choices…why did they drive into a blinding snowstorm…why didn't they pull over and park it…why didn't they stay home?"

But what about your future, the future of your community, the future of your state, and ultimately, the future of your country—if you don't get to see a forecast about the "Perfect Storm Descending upon America" in the form of endless immigration?

Sheer Enormity of the Immigration Storm

In this book, you will see exactly what you and your family face in the next three decades from the storm of "endless immigration" brought to you by your U.S. Congress, your senators, your House reps and ultimately, the president of the United States.

While no one can change the weather, each of us can change the future of our country by stopping the "immigration tsunami" bearing down on all 50 states.

As a forecaster, I can tell you this: once this immigration storm hits, no one escapes its accelerating and multiple consequences.

The 1965 Immigration Reform Act drives this "perfect storm" bearing down on the USA. At that time, Congress increased legal immigration from 200,000 annually to 1.2 million annually. That single act added 100 million people to the USA in 45 years. If allowed to continue, it will add 100 million more people within 29 years.

Let's look at the numbers. According to the Pew Research Center, NumbersUSA.org, U.S. Census Bureau and the Fogel/Martin Population Projections—legal immigration expects to jump U.S. population by 100 million people, net gain by 2050 or sooner. That includes immigrants, their birth rates and their chain-migrated relatives. The other 30 million will be U.S. births by U.S. mothers at two children per woman on average. The baseline population reached 300 million in 2006.

Dr. Steve Camarota of the Center for Immigration Studies tells us that 500,000 illegal aliens violate our borders annually. If you take 29 years times 500,000 people, that adds another 15 million more people. That would take us from the projected 439 million to 454 million in 2050. (Source: www.cis.org)

That equates to doubling the size of our 35 most populated cities within the United States. That means New York City jumps from 8.3 million to 16.6 million; Los Angeles increases from 11 million to 22 million; Chicago area from 4.0 million to 8.0 million and on down the line.

Florida expects to jump from 21 million to 33 million. Texas increases from 26 million to 36 million. California accelerates from 39 million to 58 million.

How do you water, feed, warm, transport, house, provide jobs in an increasingly robotic world, and provide resources for in excess of another 154 million people?

Given all the problems we face today such as 40 million Americans subsisting on food stamps, or 12 million unemployed (as of October 2020), or our inner cities rotting into chaos, or our air pollution rates exploding off the charts, or our gridlock traffic immobilizing our cities, or our water pollution like Flint, Michigan and dozens of other U.S. cities—how in the living daylights will we survive the first part of this storm?

My longtime colleague, the late Dr. Albert Bartlett said, "Can you think of any problem in any area of human endeavor on any scale from microscopic to global, whose long-term solution is in any demonstrable way aided, assisted or advanced by further increases of population, locally, nationally or globally?"

Of course, the answer: nothing will get better. Everything will get worse. No one will be immune. Everyone will suffer.

CHAPTER 24

//

SOCIOLOGICAL IMPACT

"It is my hypothesis that the fundamental source of conflict in this new world will not be primarily ideological or primarily economic. The great divisions among humankind and the dominating source of conflict will be cultural. Nation-states will remain the most powerful actors in world affairs, but the principal conflicts of global politics will occur between nations and groups of different civilizations. (Inside those nation states) The clash of civilizations will dominate global politics. The fault lines between civilizations will be the battle lines of the future." Samuel P. Huntington, Clash of Civilizations

As an American living in a high speed, highly technological society— how would you respond when all of a sudden someone flies you out of your home and transports you to an African village in Sudan or Somalia? What if a plane lifted you out of Chicago, Illinois and transported you to Calcutta, India?

What would you do when you arrived? First of all, no housing, no toilets, no safe food and no clean water! No jobs, no familiarity with a radically different culture and no ability to speak the language. No matter how smart, old or skilled, you would not recover from the shock of being injected into a third world society. You would huddle with your own until rescued. But if not rescued, you would live in oblivion.

Fast forward: what if you were a Somalian, Sudanese, Ethiopian or Congolese citizen transported by the U.S. Government to save you from starvation and war? You arrive in America with no skills, no job, no education, no language ability and a culture diametrically opposed to your own.

Once in America, because you lack any qualifications for work, you enjoy free food, free housing, free medical, free education, free car, free gasoline, free clothing—all paid for by working Americans who didn't ask for your burden.

From there, your kids fail in school because educational standards run beyond their intellectual horsepower. You combat new ideas of women's rights, free choice of religion, free speech and try to cope with living in an ultra-high-speed society. Because you lack skills, educational abilities and a comprehension of American culture—you live in enclaves with your fellow immigrants and become permanent wards of the state. Today, legal immigrants cost American taxpayers $113,000,000,000.00 annually with no end in sight. (Source: www.fairus.org)

Also, this fact must be realized: today, American industry robotizes redundant jobs at an astounding rate of speed. Robots make fast food completely without human hands. Automobile lines complete a car 90 percent by robots. Machines plant and harvest nearly everything going to market.

Let's look ahead to 29 years from now if the U.S. Government continues the 1965 Immigration Reform Act that brings in 100,000 unskilled refugees every 30 days and 1.5 to 1.7 million legal and illegal refugees annually. In the next 29 years, that equates to our country adding 100,000,000 legal immigrants from 190 different countries with 190 different world views. That means we import 100 million people with 190 different cultures, 190 different religions and 190 different languages. What do you think will happen with that situation?

Such an experiment could be analogous to a bunch of high school kids attending a chemistry class when the teacher exited for a call from the principal. For kicks, they threw a bunch of chemicals into a beaker to see what would happen. It could either melt down or blow up. Such an experiment proved dangerous for them, and such an experiment is proving dangerous for America, Canada, Australia and Europe.

On our current path, we will cram them into America in three short decades—so fast that they cannot and will not assimilate. They form tribal enclaves like Minneapolis, Minnesota where 120,000 Somali immigrants created "Somaliland" where Americans avoid them. The majority of them exist on permanent welfare. Additionally, Dearbornistan, Michigan with 300,000 Middle Eastern immigrants where Arabic dominates, and schools teach out of the Quran and do not subscribe to anything American. Additionally, the majority live on welfare. (Source: www.detroitnews.com, 300,000 Syrian, Lebanese, Jordanians, and Yemeni.)

Welcome to Dearborn, Michigan.

https://www.youtube.com/watch?+feature=youtu.be&v=w5oLoW9jZJc&app=desktop

Yet, the United Nations, Lutheran Churches, Catholic Churches and others force those refugees into every town that features a welfare office—knowing full well those refugees cannot and will not become functioning parts of the American workforce. And worse, those organizations understand that such places like Africa, India and Indochina continue adding 83,000,000 new babies, net gain, annually—so the line of refugees never ends.

Again, view this video to see uselessness of endless immigration. It solves nothing, but in fact exacerbates population growth:

In a five minute astoundingly simple yet brilliant video, "**Immigration, Poverty, and Gum Balls**", Roy Beck, director of www.numbersusa.ORG, graphically illustrates the impact of overpopulation. Take five minutes to see for yourself:

http://www.youtube.com/watch?v=LPjzfGChGIE&feature=player_embedded

As you can see from the video, no amount of immigration will solve the starvation, misery, suffering or hopelessness of people around the world.

But on a sociological level, America, Europe, Canada and Australia find their countries becoming "Everybody Else's Countries." Whether it's the impact of cultural conflict, religious conflict or linguistic chaos—first world countries will not survive the "Clash of Civilizations."

As stated, all cultures and ethnic groups compete for dominance. With 100 million added immigrants from 190 different countries by 2050, the USA finds those millions pulling for their own culture, ethos, language and religions. America today, already fractures and fragments in the big cities with Black Panthers and Black Lives Matter calling for a separate Black Country. With the advent of more Islamic terrorists, you will see them demanding Islamic caliphates within the USA much like Europe. Read the compelling book: **The Strange Death of Europe: Immigration, Islam, Identity** by Douglas Murray. It will give you a chilling taste of what's coming to America.

Our country faces ultimately pulling apart at the seams. We will not be able to hold in the center as "Americans."

Any culture that will not defend itself against displacement through mass immigration faces extinction. That includes both time-tested and successful cultures. Embracing diversity results in cultural suicide. America's multicultural path guarantees its destruction via cultural clashes and conflict with Islam, Mexican and African cultures that diametrically oppose American culture.

The more diverse a country, the more destructive and broken-down its future. The more people, the more it destroys its quality of life and standard of living. The more it adds immigrants, the more destruction to its environment. The more it imports refugees, the faster America, Canada, Europe and Australia lose their own ability to function and worse, their identities. Exponential growth of any civilization leads to ultimate collapse. You see it in Africa, India and China today. You will see it in Europe, Canada, Australia and America in the coming years, "IF" Western countries don't stop all forms of immigration.

CHAPTER 25

///

ENVIRONMENTAL IMPACT

"Overpopulation is the problem of the third and fourth World; over-consumption is the problem of the West. The average American child this year will consume as much of the world's resources as twenty children born in India. Deliberate and calculated waste is the central aspect of the American economy. We over-eat, over-buy, and over-build, spewing out our toxic wastes upon the earth and into the air."
Richard Foster

If we, the citizens of the United States, fail to change course by our actions, what you see in the graphs and the numbers—will occur within the next 29 years. If we don't rescind the 1965 Immigration Reform Act, yes, we are doomed to add a total of 100 million more people on our way to 625 million within 79 years. Let's figure out how to change that future.

Jacques Cousteau inspired me to start scuba diving back in 1963. He remains one of my environmental heroes.

"We must alert and organize the world's people to pressure world leaders to take specific steps to solve the two root causes of our environmental crises – exploding population growth and wasteful consumption of irreplaceable resources. Over-consumption and overpopulation underlie every environmental problem we face today." Jacques-Yves Cousteau, Oceanographer

Cousteau spelled it out clearly. But he's not alone. Another 100 top world experts say the same thing in their own books published in the past 40 years. Yet, world leaders ignore this issue like the Bubonic plague. Why?

That's the mystery of the century. Somehow, the world's elites think none of the consequences will reach them. They would be exceedingly incorrect.

As our immigration-driven population juggernaut smashes into our country by 2050, we cannot change it at that point. We face devolving into an overpopulated country. Worse, we face the "energy slave" oil exhausting by mid-century. Oil drives everything.

It's also destroying everything with carbon footprint heating up and acidifying our oceans. Why don't the elites understand that?

What's the big deal environmentally? We exhaust billions of tons of particulate and carbon that soaks into the ground and absorbs into the oceans. It kills the soil and contaminates the seven seas. Experts tell us that humans expect to burn nearly 200,000,000 barrels of oil daily by 2030—scant nine years from now. How? China adds 27 million new cars, net gain annually. Experts tell us that China will burn 98 million barrels of oil daily by 2030. (Source: **The Long Emergency** by James Howard Kunstler)

Can you imagine what's going to happen when we don't have gasoline to fill the tractors to plant crops? Harvest crops? Transport food to your table? How about the results with 8.3 million hungry people in New York City that will double to 16.6 million by 2050? What about eleven million people in Los Angeles that doubles to 22 million? How about another four million people in Chicago that jumped to eight million within 29 years?

Remember: legal immigration drives this nightmare. Illegal will add many more millions.

Do you honestly think we will be able to solve all our environmental problems with another 100 million more people? How about fresh water? Seven states already face water shortages. How about quality of life in our cities as 35 of them double their populations? What about species extinctions in the USA from habitat loss?

As Florida jumps from 21.5 million to its 33 million people by 2050, how do we solve extinction rates of alligators, puma lions, snakes, butterflies, eagles, egrets, pelicans and marsh hawks?

You got any ideas?

"At this point, it's almost certainly too late to manage a transition to sustainability on a global or national scale, even if the political will to attempt it existed, which it clearly does not. Our civilization is in the early stages of the same curve of decline and fall as so many others have followed before it. What likely lies in wait for us is a long, uneven decline into a new Dark Age. We are strong and adaptable animals and can certainly make a new life on the hotter Earth, but there will only be a fraction of inhabitable land left. There will be great clamor from climate refugees seeking a safe haven in those few parts where the climate is tolerable and food available. We will need a new set of rules for limiting the population in climate oases." James Lovelock, **The Vanishing Face of Gaia: A Final Warning**

While the media portrays the "symptoms", the cause and connection escapes them. Ironically, that "cause" escapes every national leader from the president, congressional members, and state governors—right down to average citizens.

Population equates to a mathematical problem. It is possessed of that same beautiful, and sometimes deadly, precision that we find in $E=MC^2$ and $a^2 + b^2 = c^2$. Presently, it may still be subject to our control, but with the passage of time without understanding and action will move it beyond our reach and authority. Let's begin a national conversation on immigration and a sustainable future for our children.

One final note on our dilemma: even at 2.0 children per woman on average in the USA, if we stopped all immigration, we would still add 35 million more Americans, net gain, by 2050 from "population momentum." That many more people will become an extraordinary challenge to our food production, water availability and resource base.

CHAPTER 26

///

ADDING NUMBERS THAT DON'T ADD UP ECONOMICALLY

"When the last tree is cut, the last fish is caught, and the last river is polluted; when to breathe the air is sickening, you will realize, too late, that wealth is not in bank accounts and that you can't eat money."
Alanis Obomsawim

Every Added Person Creates Added Consequences to American Society

A recent Seattle Times op-ed said that Washington State's (illegal) immigrants were "indispensable." In other words, we need our 21st century slave labor in order to ensure that our corporations make obscene profits to the detriment of our own citizens—as well as the slave wages for the illegal migrants.

Ironically, the Seattle Times did not mention that tens of thousands of Washington State citizens languish in food kitchens, food stamp and unemployment lines. They didn't mention that 6,000 Seattle homeless live in tent cities under the expressways around the city. I witnessed them during my bicycle trip along the West Coast in 2018.

Back in Colorado, in 2013, I wrote my U.S. Senator Bennet and the staff urging him to introduce a bill to reduce all legal immigration into the United States to 100,000 a year. I supplied facts, figures and graphs to support my stance. For example: we import 1.2 million legal immigrants annually while we suffer 20 million unemployed Americans. Not only can we NOT employ 20 million (at the time) of our own citizens, how do we create jobs for 1.5 million more immigrants annually with credentials only to drive a taxi or clean hotel rooms?

A sixth grader could ingest the facts and figures to see that continued mass immigration into the United States cannot be sustained from a simple jobs standpoint.

However, Bennet responded, "In regards to your recommendations, I do not believe it is in the best interest of the United States to limit legal immigration to 100,000 individuals annually. It will also place America at a competitive disadvantage moving forward. For that reason, I do not support eliminating the H-1B and H-2B Visas. I believe that these visas have the ability to benefit American companies and the economy as a whole."

Point in fact, those visas displaced 1.1 million American IT workers with foreign workers in our own country! Thanks to you, Senator Bennet and your colleagues in Congress!

In other words, to Bennet, a college graduate and who also earned a doctorate, with 12 million unemployed Americans in 2021, it's 'competitive' to add another 1.5 million legal and illegal immigrants annually. Even former Governor Lamm of Colorado said, "Are we in dreamland? The United States has had zero net job growth since 2000, yet we imported 10 million permanent immigrants in the same period. Our real U.S. unemployment rate is 17.3 percent when we consider the discouraged workers, more than 20 million, and yet the majority in Congress along with Bennet, propose increasing legal immigration and giving amnesty to millions of illegal immigrants, who themselves will be allowed to bring in their spouses, parents, children, brothers and sisters, and children of brothers and sisters. America has its plate full putting our own workers back to work."

The Numbers Collide with Reality

In a brilliant essay, Richard Pelto, "Is immigration indispensable?", Vol. 1, fall 2009, he wrote, "At a time when it is imperative to understand what is cracking the foundations of our economic and social system, Jayapal and Sinclair blindly pursue an immigration policy that demands that the now top-heavy and wobbly economic structure — already straining to remain balanced under the weight of unsustainability — be built even higher while blindly being rooted in the premise that we can never exhaust this Earth's resources. That is especially absurd because it ignores the welfare of future generations." (Source: www.thesocialcontract.com)

What astounds me as I research for my weekly columns, stems from the fact that our leaders from U.S. Senators like Bennet and Colorado's U.S. Senator John Hickenklooper—fail to understand basic arithmetic.

How can they think it's 'competitive' to inject over 100,000 immigrants every 30 days into this country, when we suffer 12 million unemployed Americans? Another 38 million Americans subsist on food stamps! Millions more suffer foreclosed homes because they cannot pay the mortgages because they don't have jobs. How about 13 million of our children living in poverty? How about 1.5 million homeless Americans? Over 60,000 Americans live in tent cities in Los Angeles and 11,000 homeless in San Francisco. Where is the logic? Where is the common sense? What planet do they live on?

Am I obtuse to ask these questions? Or, are they totally out of touch with reality as they import 1.5 million more people into this country annually? I am a former math/science teacher. Numbers either add up or they do not add up. At our current immigration rates, we can expect 100 million more immigrants injected into this country within 29 years. It's the most ignored and avoided issue in the immigration debate.

Legal Immigration Is Worse Than Illegal Because It Continues Methodically And Without Pause

To follow up on that communication with Bennet in 2013, I visited his office to present my program: "The Coming Population Crisis in America: and how to change course." In 2013, I recommended he introduce a bill to drastically cut all immigration down to 100,000 annually. I gave his entire staff the facts, figures and graphs. We could not sustain the projected 100 million added people by 2050. What did he do? He wrote Senate Bill 744 with his "Gang of Eight" to not only give amnesty to all 25 million illegal migrants, but to DOUBLE legal immigration to 2.0 million annually.

I called his staff member in the Denver office, "What didn't you understand about my presentation in your office?"

She replied, "Mr. Bennet felt like this was our best option; so, he's going to stick with the increase."

I replied, "Do you realize that you just condemned your children to an unsustainable future that will ultimately collapse our civilization by the time they reach your age?"

She said, "Well, Senator Bennet feels this is the best option."

I hung up in total shock at such utter incompetence in the face of facts I had presented.

Later, Senate Bill 744 passed the U.S. Senate, but failed in the House of Representatives.

What it showed me: we are being led by intellectual idiots who pretend to know what they are doing, but even PhD's like Bennet lack common sense and simple mathematical comprehension to make reasonable decisions. In other words, there are a lot of stupid people out there pretending to be intelligent.

CHAPTER 27

TRAGEDY OF THE COMMONS

"If the planet were a patient, we would have treated her long ago. You, ladies and gentlemen, have the power to put her on life support, and you must surely start the emergency procedures without further procrastination. Humanity faces many threats, but none is greater than climate change. In damaging our climate, we are becoming the architects of our own destruction. We have the knowledge, the tools and the money." Prince Charles of Great Britain

As the late sociologist and famous biologist Dr. Garrett Hardin said, "By any reasonable standards, the most rapidly growing populations on earth today are the most miserable."

While the citizens of those countries live in the squalor of their own numbers and collide with reality, Americans and other first world countries do not possess a clue as to the raging battle for life going on with one-third of humanity. That's more than 2.0 billion people! It's as if 9.0 million people don't die from starvation annually—but the fact is, they do!

Dr. Garrett Hardin wrote about a phenomenon that we all face. "We may well call it 'the tragedy of the commons'."

This unkind tragic destiny can only be illustrated in terms of human life by incidents which in fact involve unhappiness.

"The tragedy of the commons develops in this way," Hardin said. "Picture a pasture open to all. It is to be expected that each herdsman will try to keep as many cattle as possible on the commons. Such an arrangement may work reasonably satisfactorily for centuries because tribal wars, poaching, and disease keep the numbers of both man and beast well below the carrying capacity of the land. Finally, however, comes the day of reckoning, that is, the day when the long-desired goal of social stability becomes a reality. At this point, the inherent logic of the commons remorselessly generates tragedy."

As a competing human being, each herdsman seeks to maximize his gain. In 2021, capitalism generates maximum use of the commons, and in fact, overshoots the "commons"' ability to function…which ultimately leads to collapse. Explicitly, or implicitly, more or less consciously, the herdsman asks, "What is the utility to me of adding one more animal to my herd?" This utility has one negative and one positive component.

1) The positive component is the function of the increment of one animal. Since the herdsman receives all the proceeds from the sale of the additional animal, the positive utility is nearly +1.

2) The negative component is a function of the additional overgrazing created by one more animal. Since, however, the effects of overgrazing are shared by all the herdsmen, the negative utility for any particular decision-making herdsman is only a fraction of one.

Adding together the component partial utilities, the rational herdsman concludes that the only sensible course for him to pursue is to add another animal to his herd. And another, and another! But this is the conclusion reached by each and every rational herdsman sharing a commons. ***Therein lies the tragedy.*** Each man is locked into a system that compels him to increase his herd without limit-in a finite world. Via 21st century capitalism, consummate destruction is the destination toward which all men rush, each pursuing his own best interest in a society that believes in the freedom of the commons. Freedom in a commons brings ruin to all.

Another analogy I like to use: take a 100 gallon water tank and place it in a 50 acre pasture with two horses. They can graze, drink, romp and poop all they want. The rains keep the grass growing and the manure absorbs into the soil, thus nourishing more grass.

As soon as you add 200 horses to the 50 acre pasture, they overrun the water tank, graze the grass down to nothing, poop all over the place and destroy the carrying capacity of a limited amount of land. Perfect example of the "tragedy of the commons", "overshoot", "exceeding carrying capacity." Ultimately, everyone loses.

If you look at America today or any massively overpopulated country like China, India, Great Britain, Mexico, Bangladesh, Pakistan, Indonesia, etc., you can see the quickening of the "tragedy of the commons." You will also see millions in denial of their spiraling dilemma.

As published in my second overpopulation book, **America on the Brink: The Next Added 100 Million Americans,** in our oceans, 100 million sharks suffer death at the hands of humans annually. Humans rape the oceans with drift nets and chemicals.

"The oceans of the world continue to suffer from the survival of the philosophy of the commons," Hardin said. "Maritime nations still respond automatically to the shibboleth of the "freedom of the seas."

Professing to believe in the inexhaustible resources of the oceans, they bring species after species of fish and whales closer to extinction.

The National Parks present another instance of the working out of the tragedy of the commons. At present, they are open to all, without limits. The values that visitors seek in the park are steadily eroded. Plainly, we must soon cease to treat the parks as a commons or they will be of no value to anyone.

If we add another 100 million people, our parks cannot withstand the sheer numbers, but our cities will prove even worse.

In a Reverse Manner of the Tragedy of the Commons

Dr. Garrett Hardin said, "In a reverse way, the tragedy of the commons reappears in problems of pollution. Here it is not a question of taking something out of the commons, but of putting something in such as sewage, or chemical, radioactive, and heat wastes into water; noxious and dangerous fumes into the air; and distracting and unpleasant advertising signs into the line of sight. The rational man finds that his share of the cost of the wastes he discharges into the commons is less than the cost of purifying his wastes before releasing them. Since this is true for everyone, we are locked into a system of "fouling our own nest."

The tragedy of the commons as a food basket is averted by private property, or something formally like it. But the air and waters surrounding us cannot readily be fenced, and so the tragedy of the commons as a cesspool must be prevented by different means, by laws or taxing devices that make it cheaper for the polluter to treat his pollutants than to discharge them untreated.

Indeed, our particular concept of private property, which deters us from exhausting the positive resources of the earth, favors pollution. The owner of a factory on the bank of a stream, whose property extends to the middle of the stream, often has difficulty seeing why it is not his natural right to muddy the waters flowing past his door.

How to Legislate Temperance?

Weekly newspaper and TV reports illustrate our dilemma for example: "Sixty percent in nation breathe dirty air…186 million Americans at risk," Denver Post, April 29, 2009 by Noaki Schwartz.

Yet, we ignore the core cause. We blissfully go about our business as if we cannot possibly end up like China. When you read Clugston's work, you will understand our dilemma. Our present Titanic-like course, driven by relentless immigration, must be changed. If we fail to change course, we eventually become victims.

Tragedy of the Commons as to Overpopulation

The tragedy of the commons is involved in population problems in another way.

In the past, over-breeding brought its own "punishment" to the germ line—then there would be no public interest in controlling the breeding of families. But our society is deeply committed to the welfare state, and hence is confronted with another aspect of the tragedy of the commons. For example, according to the Edwin Rubenstein report, "Illegal and legal immigration cost U.S. taxpayers $346 billion annually across 15 federal agencies." That includes education, medication, food and incarceration. (Source: www.esrresearch.com, Edwin Rubenstein Report on Immigration Costs, September 28, 2006)

In a welfare state, how shall we deal with the family, the religion, the race, or the class that adopts over-breeding as a policy to secure its own aggrandizement? To couple the concept of freedom to breed with the belief that everyone born has an equal right to the commons is to lock the world into a tragic course of action.

Conscience Is Self-Eliminating

At the present moment, Mexico, Central and South American citizens converge into America at rapid speeds from overpopulating within their own societies. Mexico boasts 15 to 28 million Mexicans living within the United States.

Today, Pakistan expects to double its population from 80 million to 160 million by mid-century. Clearly, they exceed the Commons. China adds eight million annually. India adds 14 to 16 million annually. Where do they flee?

As witnessed in this film, Middle Eastern people reached from five to seven million in the USA since 1970. They added 52 million to Europe within 40 years. They expect to be the dominant ethnic group in Europe by mid-century. Clearly, they overwhelm the commons. For a look at the "Tragedy of the Commons" consider this eight minute movie: http://www.youtube.com/watch?v=6-3X5hIFXYU

We will discover that ethnic groups will continue multiplying their numbers for a greater "share" of the commons, which translates to short term power. India illustrates that dilemma in that its many ethnic groups try to out-birth one another for more political power. Unfortunately, their misery and environmental damage accelerate with their added 16 million annually.

As the "Tragedy of the Commons" quickens, no one wins and everyone loses no matter what their race, creed or color.

Infringement of the Commons

Since Hardin wrote the "Tragedy of the Commons" in 1968, humans added another 4.3 billion to the planet. The U.S. added 130 million people. Few blink or swallow at our dilemma. Most Americans dodge, duck or avoid the population equation at every juncture—even as they watch its accelerating 'symptoms' in this country and worldwide.

Organizations feature Green Revolution, alternative energy, mass transit and conservation—but they won't touch hyper-population growth.

You must wonder why a sane man or woman would walk onto a railroad track to discover a train headed in his or her direction, but he turns around and walks the other way, so he won't see it when that locomotive runs over him. As intelligent at the United States purports to be, it follows in the same footsteps of China, Mexico, Pakistan and India's—horrific population overload.

I am waiting for a rational U.S. Senator or even the president to introduce a bill that addresses the future: "US Sustainable Population Policy", "US Carrying Capacity Policy." What does that mean? First of all, since 1970, the average woman birthed 2.03 children for a stable population. What grew us by 100 million in 56 years? Immigration! Can we continue on our current path and still survive?

Without stopping the added numbers, that population train along with the Tragedy of the Commons bears down on us with accelerating speed.

SECTION 4

COMPELLING REASONS TO CHANGE COURSE

CHAPTER 28

//

SERIOUS REALITIES FACING OUR CIVILIZATION IN THE 21ST CENTURY

"In the Amazon, you may walk for days without seeing a tree; in Beijing, the air is the color of a bruise. Three thousand miles of litter floats in the Atlantic Ocean, plastic bags and old nappies, bumping against the side of the ships. I sat before a committee in Brussels and they said, 'What do you want us to do about it? If we change now, we'll destroy our own economies." I said, 'You have destroyed your own world'" Claire North, The End of the Day

In the final analysis, this book could continue into some very heavy, if not sobering material, but for now, it gives you an idea of what this civilization faces and what we must do to change course. These final quotes give you an idea of our predicament from some of the finest minds in the world. You saw them earlier in this book, however, it's worth it to repeat in this section for easy access. These men and women speak from all walks of life.

"If we don't halt population growth with justice and compassion, it will be done for us by nature, brutally and without pity – and will leave a ravaged world." Nobel Laureate Dr. Henry W. Kendall

"It's our population growth that underlies just about every single one of the problems that we've inflicted on planet. If there were just a few of us, then the nasty things we do wouldn't really matter and Mother Nature would take care of it, but there are so many of us, way too many of us." Jane Goodall, PhD, DBE

121

"The raging monster upon the land is population growth. In its presence, sustainability is but a fragile theoretical construct. To say, as many do, that the difficulties of nations are not due to people, but to poor ideology and land-use management is sophistic." Harvard scholar and biologist E.O. Wilson

"Most Western elites continue urging the wealthy West not to stem the migrant tide [that adds 80 million net gain annually to the planet], but to absorb our global brothers and sisters until their horrid ordeal has been endured and shared by all—ten billion humans packed onto an ecologically devastated planet." Dr. Otis Graham, **Unguarded Gates**

"We are either going to have a future where women lead the way to make peace with the Earth or we are not going to have a human future at all." Vandana Shiva

"Somehow, we have come to think the whole purpose of the economy is to grow, yet growth is not a goal or purpose. The pursuit of endless growth is suicidal." David Suzuki

"We will not go back to normal. Normal never was. Our pre-corona existence was not normal other than we normalized greed, inequity, exhaustion, depletion, extraction, disconnection, confusion, rage, hoarding, hate and lack. We are given the opportunity to stitch a new garment. One that fits all of humanity and nature." Sonya Taylor

"We are headed for a catastrophic temperature rise of 3-5C this century. Making peace with nature is the defining task of the 21st century. It must be the top priority for everyone, everywhere." António Guterres, secretary general of the United Nations

"What is acted out on the female body parallels the larger practices of domination, fragmentation, and conquest against the earth body, which is being polluted, strip-mined, deforested, and cut up into parcels of private property. Equally, this pattern points to the fragmentation of the psyche, which ultimately underlies and enables all of this damage." Jane Caputi

"Growth for the sake of yet more growth is a bankrupt and eventually lethal idea. CASSE is the David fighting the Goliath of endless expansion, and we know how that one turned out." David Orr

The green revolution was instigated as a result of the efforts of Norman Borlaug, who, while accepting the Nobel Peace Prize in 1970, said, "The green revolution has won a temporary success in man's war against hunger and deprivation; it has given man a breathing space. If fully implemented, the revolution can provide sufficient food for sustenance during the next three decades. But the frightening power of human reproduction must also be curbed; otherwise, the success of the green revolution will be ephemeral only."

"Women must see that there can be no liberation for them and no solution to the ecological crisis within a society whose fundamental model of relationships continues to be one of domination. They must unite the demands of the women's movement with those of the ecological movement to envision a radical reshaping of the basic socioeconomic relations and the underlying values of this [modern industrial] society." Rosemary Radford Ruether

"The cheap oil age created an artificial bubble of plentitude for a period not much longer than a human lifetime....so I hazard to assert that as oil ceases to be cheap and the world reserves move toward depletion, we will be left with an enormous population...that the ecology of the earth will not support. The journey back toward non-oil population homeostasis will not be pretty. We will discover the hard way that population hyper growth was simply a side-effect of the oil age. It was a condition, not a problem with a solution. That is what happened, and we are stuck with it." James Howard Kunstler, **The Long Emergency**

"We must alert and organize the world's people to pressure world leaders to take specific steps to solve the two root causes of our environmental crises – exploding population growth and wasteful consumption of irreplaceable resources. Over-consumption and overpopulation underlie every environmental problem we face today." Jacques-Yves Cousteau, Oceanographer

"Upwards of two hundred species…mostly of the large, slow-breeding variety…are becoming extinct here every day because more and more of the earth's carrying capacity is systematically being converted into human carrying capacity. These species are being burnt out, starved out, and squeezed out of existence…thanks to technologies that most people, I'm afraid, think of as technologies of peace. I hope it will not be too long before the technologies that support our population explosion begin to be perceived as no less hazardous to the future of life on this planet than the endless production of radioactive wastes." Daniel Quinn

"Because people and especially men feel superior, the environment, animals or women can be exploited." Emilie Hache

"We've poured our poisons into the world as though it were a bottomless pit. and we go on gobbling them up. It's hard to imagine how the world could survive another century of this abuse, but nobody's really doing anything about it. It's a problem our children will have to solve, or their children." Daniel Quinn

"As we go from this happy hydrocarbon bubble we have reached now to a renewable energy resource economy, which we do this century, will the "civil" part of civilization survive? As we both know there is no way that alternative energy sources can supply the amount of per capita energy we enjoy now, much less for the 9 billion expected by 2050. And energy is what keeps this game going. We are involved in a Faustian bargain— selling our economic souls for the luxurious life of the moment, but sooner or later the price has to be paid." Walter Youngquist, **Geodestinies**

"This earth is my sister; I love her daily grace, her silent daring, and how loved I am. How we admire this strength in each other, all that we have lost, all that we have suffered, all that we know. We are stunned by this beauty, and I do not forget: what she is to me, what I am to her." Susan Griffin

"The U.S. will set a record in the rate of rise—and fall of an empire. Between wide open borders and fall of the dollar and growing population against a declining resource base, the US will be defeated from within. Mobs will rule the streets in the nation that is now the third largest in the world and unable to support its population except by taking resources from other countries." Arnold Toynbee, historian

"A simple look at the upward path of global greenhouse emissions indicates we will continue to squeeze the trigger on the gun we have put to our own head." Eugene Linden, **The Winds of Change: Climate, Weather and the Destruction of Civilization**

"If this world is to be healed through human efforts, I am convinced it will be by ordinary people whose love for life is even greater than their fear." Joanna Macy

"The ship is already starting to spin out of control. We may soon lose all chance of grabbing the wheel. Humanity faces a genuinely new situation. It is not an environmental crisis in the accepted sense. It is a crisis for the entire life-support system for our civilization and our species." Fred Pearce, **The Last Generation: How Nature Will take Her Revenge for Climate Change**

"At this point, it's almost certainly too late to manage a transition to sustainability on a global or national scale, even if the political will to attempt it existed, which it clearly does not. Our civilization is in the early stages of the same curve of decline and fall as so many others have followed before it. What likely lies in wait for us is a long, uneven decline into a new Dark Age from which, centuries from now, the civilizations of the future will gradually emerge." James Lovelock

"If present growth trends in population, industrialization, pollution, food production and resource depletion continue unchanged, the limits to growth will be reached sometime in the next 100 years." The Club of Rome 1972

"We are strong and adaptable animals and can certainly make a new life on the hotter Earth, but there will only be a fraction of inhabitable land left. Soon we face the appalling question of who can we let aboard the lifeboats? And who must we reject? There will be great clamor from climate refugees seeking a safe haven in those few parts where the climate is tolerable and food available. We will need a new set of rules for limiting the population in climate oases." James Lovelock, **The Vanishing Face of Gaia: A Final Warning**

"Imagine we live on a planet. Not our cozy, taken for granted planet, but a planet, a real one, with melting poles and dying forests and a heaving, corrosive sea, raked by winds, strafed by storms, scorched by heat. And inhospitable place. It needs a new name, Eaarth." Bill McKibben, **Eaarth: Making a Life on a Tough New Planet**

"I cannot see how we will ever come to know a primary causative factor of human population growth, much less respond ably to the climate and ecological threats resulting from that unsustainable growth, if we deny sound ecological research of human population dynamics that explains clearly why that unbridled growth continues in an unrelenting manner in our time. If we choose to ignore extant, uncontested, virtually irrefutable scientific evidence that discloses a root cause of the extraordinary increase of global human population numbers occurring on our watch, we cannot be expected to respond ably to the worldwide climate and ecological challenges that are directly precipitated by a continuously exploding human population." Steven Earl Salmony

"But man is a part of nature, and his war against nature is inevitably a war against himself. Why should we tolerate a diet of weak poisons, a home in insipid surroundings, a circle of acquaintances who are not quite our enemies, the noise of motors with just enough relief to prevent insanity? Who would want to live in a world which is just not quite fatal?" Rachel Carson, **Silent Spring**

"The power of population is so superior to the power of earth to produce subsistence to humanity that premature death must in some shape or other visit the human race." Thomas Malthus 1798

"Can you think of any problem in any area of human endeavor on any scale, from microscopic to global, whose long-term solution is in any demonstrable way aided, assisted, or advanced by further increases of population, locally, nationally, or globally." Dr. Albert Bartlett

"All causes are lost causes without limiting human population," Dr. Paul Ehrlich, Stanford University

"The weight of our civilization has become so great; it now ranks as a global force and a significant wild card in the human future along with the Ice Ages and other vicissitudes of a volatile and changeable planetary system." Dianne Dumanoski, **Rethinking Environmentalism**

"To make the changes we need to make and to reach a safer future, we will need the resources of everybody here — the scientists, the policy makers, and the industrialists — all working together towards a common goal. And that goal is a planet that can continue to support life." Dr. Piers Sellers, **American astronaut**

"Ecofeminism adds that patriarchy devalues women, and therefore devalues nature, because nature is seen as mother. Women and nature get trashed together. Anything patriarchy associates with women is also trashed: caring, compassion, mothering, emotions, looking after nature, valuing life over money. To survive the climate emergency, we need to know we're part of Mother Nature. To value nature, we must honor women too, and vice versa." Ms. Dido Dunlop

"It's going to destroy it all. I use what I call my bathroom metaphor. If two people live in an apartment, and there are two bathrooms, then both have what I call freedom of the bathroom, go to the bathroom any time you want, and stay as long as you want to for whatever you need. And this to my way is ideal. And everyone believes in the freedom of the bathroom. It should be right there in the Constitution. But if you have 20 people in the apartment and two bathrooms, no matter how much every person believes in freedom of the bathroom, there is no such thing. You have to set up, you have to set up times for each person, you have to bang at the door, aren't you through yet, and so on. And in the same way, democracy cannot survive overpopulation. Human dignity cannot survive it. Convenience and decency cannot survive it. As you put more and more people onto the world, the value of life not only declines, but it disappears. It doesn't matter if someone dies." Isaac Asimov

"I shouldn't be up here. I should be back in school on the other side of the ocean. Yet, you all come to us young people for hope. How dare you? You have stolen my dreams and my childhood with your empty words. Yet, I am one of the lucky ones. People are suffering." Greta Thunberg

"No one ever dies of overpopulation. Every event has many antecedents, and we usually attribute our problems or the occurrence of catastrophic events to the most immediate and obvious antecedents, while overlooking the role of population growth as a major driving factor in creating the conditions for the antecedent events to occur." Madeline Weld, Canada

"The truth is: the natural world is changing. And we are totally dependent on that world. It provides our food, water and air. It is the most precious thing we have, and we need to defend it." David Attenborough

CHAPTER 29

IMMIGRATION POLICY WITHOUT POPULATION POLICY ILLOGICAL

"To establish immigration policy without first establishing population policy is both illogical . . . and undemocratic!" Edward C. Hartman author of The Population Fix: Breaking America's Addiction to Population Growth.

In 1965, our U.S. Senate passed the Immigration Reform Act that changed annual migration into America from 175,000 annually to 1.2 and as high as 1.5 million immigrants from all over the world every year. Within 41 years, the United States blasted from 196 million people to 300 million in October of 2006. From that point in 1965, we added 104 million more problems to our civilization. We haven't begun to solve the problems of that many people impacting our cities, our environment and our way of life. We fantasize that our civilization can avoid the results now impacting other overpopulated countries like China, Mexico, Haiti and India.

If the 1965 immigration bill continues in place, America expects to add 100 million people by 2050 while it accelerates to over 625 million by the end of the century. Ultimately, we will exceed one billion people. If the current amnesty bill passes, another 20 to 25 million illegal alien migrants will enjoy instant citizenship, which will, in turn, allow chain migration of 10 members each of their families to add a possible total of over 100 million more people over time.

Millions of Americans line up for food at food banks daily. Over 40 million Americans subsist on food stamps. Over 13 million American children live below the poverty line. Poverty has become entrenched in

America and grows worse with endless immigration out of the third world. If you travel to San Francisco like I did last summer, you will note 11,000 people living in tents on the streets of the "City by the Bay." Another trip to Los Angeles will astound you with 62,000 people living in tents and under blue tarps as they use cardboard for mattresses. That number drops to 6,000 homeless in Seattle, Washington as of the summer of 2020. All in all, 1,000,000 Americans and thousands of veterans remain homeless while we absorb 1.5 million legal and illegal immigrants annually.

Congress passed the immigration bill without any understanding or the consequential ramifications to adding over 100 million people to the United States. They thought not one second about environmental degradation, energy depletion or resource exhaustion. They gave no thought to degraded quality of life or standard of living.

Countless Americans and illegal migrants live in tent cities and in abandoned warehouses around the United States. They lack toilets, clean water and heat. We can expect millions more as we import millions of third world refugees. We cannot keep up with the numbers nor can we provide jobs. Worse, no one possesses the money or facilities to alleviate the crisis.

Today in 2021, we drive millions of cars through toxic, air polluted cities with endless honking, sirens, concrete jungles and human compaction. We separate ourselves from nature via steel, glass and asphalt. We face endless emotional, physiological and neurological diseases engendered by fast-paced modern living.

Hartman said, "Population growth in America may not be a physiological addiction, but it has become an economic, political and psychological addiction negatively affecting virtually every American."

Millions of poverty-stricken Americans live in trailers. Two of Adell White Dog Johnson's grandchildren sleep in their strollers near their family's burned-down trailer in Eagle Butte, S.D. Adell, 45, had complained about the wiring the previous week. No one was hurt in the fire, but her family lost everything they had, including a computer they had recently bought.

Adell, who also lost her previous trailer to an electrical fire, makes less than minimum wage as a dishwasher at a local restaurant. FEMA sells Native Americans condemned trailers which are dangerous to inhabit. Residents also have little incentive to buy their own home, since it disqualifies them from receiving general assistance. The system on the reservation, created in part by the Federal Government, has created a dependent society, the antithesis of Native Americans' desire to be a self-reliant and sovereign nation.

Today, yet another U.S. Congress not only huddles to give 20 to 25 million illegal aliens instant citizenship, they may include adding another one million immigrants to the 1.2 million that already legally migrate into the USA annually.

At our current 330 million, Hartman points out our current problems:

- Rising housing prices
- Urban sprawl
- Horrifically gridlocked traffic in all our major cities
- Rising infrastructure costs and rising taxes
- Deterioration of public and social services
- Impact of massive housing developments
- Worsening air quality and water quality
- Polarizing local politics and gridlocked government
- Rising unemployment
- Spreading pavement and attendant problems with runoff
- Failing water supplies with seven states suffering water shortages
- Destruction of farmland, wilderness and rivers
- Lost quality of life

Hartman asks us to reconsider what it will be like when we reach 1.0 billion. China didn't ask the question until too late and India refuses to ask it. It shows the power of culture and religion over common sense and rational thinking.

Hartman said, "America's population pushers have a variety of motives. However, many have one trait in common: they have never asked themselves the question, 'How many Americans are enough?'"

(Source: **www.thepopulationfix.com**)

Instead, they push for "exponential growth" that leads to ultimate collapse as discussed earlier in this book. How can such persons be so myopic? You might call it our national heritage to harness capitalism, manifest destiny and a religious conviction to "go forth, multiply and take dominion over everything." Unfortunately, that makes for a deadly combination of destruction of the air, land and water.

Today, yet another 535 congressional critters huddle to expand mass immigration. Again, they lack the intellectual talent or environmental understandings to understand the impacts of millions of added people.

They prove the following statement: "The First Basic Law of Human Stupidity asserts without ambiguity: always and inevitably everyone underestimates the number of stupid individuals in circulation.

"At first, the statement sounds trivial. Closer scrutiny reveals its veracity. No matter how high are one's estimates of human stupidity, one is repeatedly startled by the fact that: people whom one had once judged rational and intelligent turn out to be unashamedly stupid. Additionally, day after day, with unceasing monotony, one is harassed in one's activities by stupid individuals who appear suddenly and unexpectedly in the most inconvenient places and at the most improbable moments." (Source: Carlo M. Cipolla, Professor of Economics, UC Berkeley)

You cannot help but scratch your head as to our ongoing folly as a civilization. It's as if we cannot help ourselves. Nonetheless, we must discover the courage and fortitude to save ourselves.

Economist Kenneth Boulding said, "Anyone who believes in indefinite growth on a physically finite planet, is either mad or an economist."

At the end of his book, Hartman offers 13 methods for you to take action. You must remember that a constitutional republic demands citizen participation. We must take action to make sure those congressional critters take the correct action. Our destiny is not a matter of chance, it's a matter of our choosing to act and fulfill a positive outcome. You cannot wait for your future to unfold positively; you must make it a positive future for yourself and your fellow creatures that share this planet with you.

Hartman urges a "U.S. Population Policy" that will move us viably into the future. We may avoid the fate of countless civilizations before us by taking action to balance our numbers with the carrying capacity of this planet.

CHAPTER 30

//

SHOULD WE HUMANS FEEL GUILTY FOR OVERPOPULATING THIS PLANET?

"I hope to use my celebrity to motivate people and contribute to moving our global society back from the brink. I am surprised environment is not at the top of the agenda. What is more important than good, clean air?" Don Cheadle, Actor & UN Environment Goodwill Ambassador

Recently, one of my ardent readers said, "Humans should not feel guilty about living on Earth...." He defended humanity's overpopulation running roughshod over the planet and the oceans. He defended that humans own the right to reproduce themselves forever. He argued that we can add another 20, 30 and 40 billion people to the planet without consequences. He felt that our causing the extinction of over 100 species daily cannot be our concern. In other words: he lacks the intellectual horsepower to understand his own dilemma.

A recent commentary in the Wall Street Journal by Jonathan Last advocated for more babies along with other writers like Joel Kotkin, Megan McArdle and Justin Green. One author wrote, **One Billion Americans: The Case for Thinking Bigger** by Mathew Iglesais. The book received over 100 five-star ratings. The book stands as a hallmark for human stupidity at its highest. Yet, they enjoy major front-page advocacy support for population growth. All the while, our planet reels, staggers and lurches with humanity's siege of the biosphere from accelerating carbon footprint, ecological footprint, acidified oceans, climate destabilization, horrendous species extinctions, Great Pacific Garbage Patch and 20,000 square mile dead zones at the mouths of rivers worldwide.

A hundred years ago, Alfred Whitehead in his "Adventures of Ideas", made a statement that spelled out a logical path for the advancement of the human race: **"The foundation of all understanding...is that no static maintenance of perfection is possible. This axiom is rooted in the nature of life. Advance or decay are the only choices offered humanity. The pure conservative is fighting against the essence of the universe."**

Whitehead said that we must change our thinking to fit new realities. We must take Galileo's new understandings that the Earth no longer enjoys the universe revolving around it, but in fact, our planet remains a speck in the black void of eternity. This planet remains finite with a finite carrying capacity. Humans, to be sure, need to get a clue that they are not God's gift to the world. In fact, Shim Schimmel, the renowned artist said, "With creatures like human beings, even the stars aren't safe."

With more intelligent Americans surveyed recently, they were asked the question: Do Americans think stabilizing population will help protect the environment? Fifty-four percent believe stabilization will. As you finish this book, you might feel that 100 percent need to vote for stabilization of our population.

My friend Steve Kurtz said, "Nothing on Earth happens in a vacuum. It's a closed system that begins to buckle under the sheer weight of human demands. Scientists are increasingly linking population growth and overconsumption to our environmental challenges."

With my six continents of bicycle travel, I unequivocally understand and have seen firsthand that human overpopulation accelerates as the single most dangerous issue facing humanity and all life on this planet in the 21st century.

In just the past few years, scientists have found in America:

- The Colorado River system is under assault by a growing population, and there are serious doubts it can meet the West's demand for water in the coming decades.
- Florida's aquifer, the water supply for 21.5 million people, is experiencing saltwater intrusion because of over-pumping.

- The United States will lose 36 million acres of forest to urban sprawl by 2050.
- Sixty-six species of coral should be classified as endangered because population and consumption of resources are a driving factor in the threats they face.
- The Gunnison sage grouse merits endangered-species protection in part because the human population has doubled in its habitat and will double again in the next 20 years.
- Florida panthers experienced the second year in a row of record-breaking road kills deaths due to increased traffic and development in panther habitat.
  - According to the Department of Interior, because of human encroachment, we lose hundreds of plants and animals to extinction in North America every decade. That number will accelerate as we race toward an added 100 million by 2050 and 625 million by the end of the century.

What's going on with our oceans defies and frightens even the "hardest" mentality: acidification of the oceans so many life forms will go extinct including our reefs. Plastic devastation like the "Great Pacific Garbage Patch" killing millions of marine and avian creatures annually. Over 20,000 square mile dead zones at the mouths of rivers around the world running raw sewage laden with chemicals 24/7. The list multiplies as we multiply.

Many Americans get it, and our leaders need to get it, and we all need to understand that we cannot stand around with our noses stuck to a TV set or a smart phone. We need to participate in our future and the future of our children.

The poll asked: if mass extinctions of plants and animals were unavoidable due to population growth, do we have a moral responsibility to address the problem? Sixty percent said "Yes!" After reading this book, I'm certain you would vote for 100 percent needing to agree with that question.

CHAPTER 31

MAN SWARM ERADICATING FELLOW SPECIES

"If global warming were held to a minimum, the team estimated that between 22 and 31 percent of the species would be "committed to extinction" by 2050. If warming were to reach what was at that point considered a likely maximum—a figure that now looks too low—by the middle of this century, between 38 and 52 percent of the species would be fated to disappear." Elizabeth Kolbert, The Sixth Extinction: An Unnatural History

Man Swarm and the Killing of Wildlife by Dave Foreman

The Bible commanded, "Be fruitful and multiply, fill the earth and subdue it and take dominion over all living things on land and in the seas."

At the time of the Bible's inception by a desert tribe known as the Jews in the Middle East, less than 100 million human beings walked the planet, give or take a few. Humans used nets and spears to subdue fish, fowl and beasts.

In 2021, as the human race thunders toward adding another three billion of its already prolific numbers to reach 10 billion by mid-century, thousands of scientists have warned of our impending predicament. Nonetheless, we human earthlings plunder oceans, seas, air, land and water.

At the same time, starvation stalks humans in Somalia, Bangladesh, Mexico, Congo, Sudan and India. Over 12 million human beings die of starvation annually around the globe. (Source: World Health Organization, UN Population stats)

But what about the other "earthlings" numbering perhaps 30 million separate species around the globe? What about their plight as humans maraud this planet by mercilessly annihilating habitat and poisoning the oceans?

How many species suffer extinction daily around the planet? Dr. Norman Myers, Oxford University, United Kingdom, substantiates 80 to 100 species end their time on this planet every day via human habitat encroachment. Humans exterminate countless species at such a prolific rate that it is deemed the "Sixth Extinction Session." The first five sessions arrived as ice ages, meteors and other deadly events.

Harvard University biologist Edward O. Wilson said, "The worst thing that will probably happen—in fact is already well underway—is not energy depletion, economic collapse, conventional war, or the expansion of totalitarian governments. As terrible as these catastrophes would be for us, they can be repaired in a few generations. The one process now going on that will take millions of years to correct is loss of genetic and species diversity by the destruction of natural habitats. This is the folly our descendants are least likely to forgive us."

Long time environmental activist Dave Foreman wrote a penetrating and compelling book: **Man Swarm and the Killing of Wildlife.** This book cannot be dismissed. It cannot be ignored. It cannot be put down once started. Foreman shows the unraveling of the wild world at the hands of humanity. For anyone that thinks unlimited human growth can continue, this book knocks out all the myths perpetrated by economists, religious leaders and pro-growth advocates.

Foreman dedicates his book to his friend Hugh Iltis, "Whose stout heart and sharp mind has always seen that the population explosion leads to the death of wild things and the loss of wilderness."

In my own media battles on the population, immigration, and the environmental front, I have had to contend with big time radio talk show hosts who support unlimited growth, but also report about the consequences—never making the connection. Newspapers like the Denver Post, New York Times, Boston Globe and Washington Post remain convinced that unlimited growth benefits everyone.

The Los Angeles Times encourages as much growth as possible even as California chokes on its toxic air, gridlocked highways and crumbling infrastructure. It adds 1,655 people daily, net gain, along with 400 vehicles. Even small-town newspaper editors like Jonathan Thompson of the High Country News advocate for unlimited growth. (Source: www.capsweb.org)

National Public Radio hosts avoid the topic at all costs. Terry Gross, Steve Inskeep, Robert Siegel, Liane Hanson and others skirt the population topic like the plague. Only a few years ago Thomas Friedman wrote: **The Earth Is Flat**, but he advocated for a better energy source in order to keep growing. I wrote a scathing review of his book and his thinking on Amazon.

Friedman's book didn't make a dent. I've written 150 similar commentaries over the past 20 years. To give you a more sobering perspective, the USA adds 8,100 people net gain daily while the planet hosts another 240,000 new babies, net gain, 24/7.

From my own work, **I unequivocally state that human overpopulation in America and around the world is the most avoided, ignored and suppressed issue of our time. It's also the most dangerous predicament of our time, but don't let that stop us from increasing our numbers at rapid speed.**

While you may hear a lot about "carrying capacity", you never hear about carrying capacity for all the other creatures on our planet. It's like they don't exist or are unimportant. Foreman loves wild things and I love them, too.

Foreman wrote, "We have come on like a swarm of locusts: a wide, thick, darkling cloud settling down like living snowflakes, smothering every stalk, every leaf, eating away every scrap of green down to raw, bare wasting earth. It's painfully straightforward. There are too many humans for Earth to harbor…we are crippling Earth's life support system by such a flood of upright apes devouring the land."

Dave Foreman's book will rock your senses. Everything he addresses will negatively impact your children. It will change all life on this planet if humans continue their endless onslaught around the globe.

100 years of human progress caused massive animal extinction rates

Could you do without the grizzly bear, leopard, cougar, deer, elk, hummingbird, Canada goose, fox, prairie dog, bald eagle, trout, whale, sharks and a vast array of the animal kingdom? Would you like to see them completely disappear because they are not important?

If you do, you may get your wish in the 21st century as humanity continues its onslaught of wilderness habitat around the world. As the human mob rockets past 7.8 billion people, all plant and animal life on this planet stands in the cross hairs of extinction.

This book cannot be dismissed. It cannot be ignored. It cannot be put down once started. Foreman shows the unraveling of the wild world at the hands of humanity. But he also presents solutions to save the animals and ultimately, human beings.

The legendary environmentalist John Muir said, "When you pick up a rock, you realize that it is hitched to everything else in the universe."

That means water, soil, air, wind, sun and fire hitch themselves to humans, plants and animals. Conversely, we hitch ourselves to all living creatures and non-living things on this planet. We cannot get away from it: we remain a part of the web of life.

Aldo Leopold said, "There are those who can live without wild things and there are those who cannot."

You have to wonder if all those pill-popping and booze guzzling city slickers suffering from concrete below their feet and glass and steel in their eyes daily—wouldn't find a bit of wilderness a welcome respite to the un-natural settings of the cities where most Americans live in the 21st century.

Muir added, "Tell me what you will of the benefactions of city civilization, of the sweet security of streets—all as part of the natural up-growth of man towards the high destiny we hear so much of. I know that our bodies were made to thrive only in pure air, and the scenes in which pure air is found. If the death exhalations that brood the broad towns in which we so fondly compact ourselves were made visible, we should flee as from a plague. All are more or less sick; there is not a perfectly sane man in all of San Francisco." September 1874.

You can imagine the compounding of the emotional, spiritual and mental sicknesses going on in our major cities today where everyone suffers compacted living, projects, gridlock, overcrowded schools and highly stressed people in every sector of life?

Foreman exposes the factors that humans face as we continue to grow our numbers. "More of our kind equates to fewer wild things…a stabilized human population means hope for wild things. A shrinking human population means a better world for wild things. And for men and women and children."

Foreman states that he will educate readers as to the population explosion accelerating in the United States and worldwide. He wants you to understand that it is the main driver for current extinction rates— off the charts. He exposes *cornucopians* who advocate for endless human population growth. Finally, he offers solutions.

But we better get to them fast! Eminent Harvard biologist E.O. Wilson said, "By the end of the century half of all species will be extinct. Does that matter?"

You better understand that it does matter! Wilson also said, "If all mankind were to disappear, the world would regenerate back to the rich state of equilibrium that existed ten thousand years ago. If insects were to vanish, the environment would collapse into chaos."

Foreman said, "Today's 'Sixth Extinction Session' features humans as a living scythe with which to mow down life on Earth. One species. Homo sapiens. Humans. That's us!"

The human race broke out of the "Circle of Life" to become the most destructive species ever encountered on the planet. **No other creature has created 84,000 chemical poisons that undermine all life forms. No other species has changed the "pH" of the oceans in so short a time. No other creature has scavenged the resources in a blind lust for things.**

Can the planet balance our poisons to continue supporting all life?

Foreman issues the famous I=PAT equation. The impact of any human group on the environment can be usefully viewed as the product of three different factors. "P" is for population. "A" stands for affluence or usage of resources. "T" stands technologies disrupting the natural work of nature.

"Unlike most books that have warned of overpopulation," said Foreman, "I will spend little time on tales about coming starvation, breakdown of civilization, running out of oil and wars over dwindling raw goods. I will center on the most dreadful and unforgivable outcome of Man's population explosion and that is what we are doing to our fellow Earthlings."

Destructive momentum: can enlightened environmentalist overcome global pollution, climate destabilization, species extinction?

The late William R. Catton, author of **Overshoot,** explained that humanity exceeded the carrying capacity of the planet decades ago. Our species lives in "overshoot" otherwise what might be considered as borrowed time.

"Human actions have been undoing much of what the biosphere offers to make this planet suitable to support a quality of human life," said Catton. "A growing number of humans, equipped with resource-ravenous technology, have exploited a widening array of natural resources, both renewable and non-renewable. Ideas about limits are now vital."

Scarcity: Humanity's Final Chapter by Christopher O. Clugston chronicles our destruction and exhaustion of non-renewable resources.

We rapidly exhaust the metals, minerals and materials that run our computers, cell phones, batteries, solar panels and thousands of other products. As we humans continue exploding our numbers, Mother Earth cannot cope with endless mining of her resources. She will run out on or before 2050.

Unfortunately, as we accelerate our human numbers, we not only exhaust Earth's resources, we impact the environment, water supplies and food available for the other creatures that share this planet with us.

Catton understood this factor in 1982 when he wrote his book, "I was already concerned that the 4.5 billion of us were seriously damaging Earth. In woeful ecological ignorance, we were failing to see the entire destiny toward which we were/are racing. We need to know that we were living by a cornucopian myth, namely the euphoric belief in limitless resources. We needed to understand that by so living we were drawing down on Earth's non-renewable resources and using the renewable resources faster than their rates of replenishment—so were stealing from posterity. We needed to know that we have grown beyond the Earth's carrying capacity."

Since that book and those words by Catton, we added another 2.5 billion people to reach our astounding 7.8 billion people scavenging this planet's limited resources.

In **Life on the Brink: Environmentalists Confront Overpopulation** by Professor Philip Cafaro of Colorado State University and Professor

Eileen Crist of Virginia Tech—we find the top scientists in the world attempting to alert humanity to its impending future viability on this planet. They learned from Catton's knowledge and they educate the reader as to what the other creatures of the planet face as we maintain our breakneck speed of human population growth.

What do we humans hope to accomplish as we continue the "Sixth Extinction Session" against the other creatures sharing this planet? How will we feel when the last Bengal tiger vanishes? Its passing will be more catastrophic than the Carrier Pigeon's demise. But what happens when the last grizzly bear gives up living on this planet? How about the last bald eagle?

This book brings those realities to your front doorstep. Right now, in America, where we pretend to push for Environmental Protection and care for National Parks and care of other species—instead, we grow our numbers and accelerate extinction rates.

Add another 100 million of us within 29 years and what do you expect to happen? How many more extinct North American animals as well as plants will result?

At some point, we humans must figure out how to stabilize our numbers so our fellow creatures stand a chance for their own survival.

"The American people today are involved in warfare more deadly than the war in Vietnam, but few of them seem aware of it and even fewer of them are doing anything about it. This is a war that is being waged against the American environment, against our lands, air, and water, which are the basis of that environment." Norman Cousins (1915-1990)

We war against the animals living in North America and around the world. It's a war that we most certainly will lose on many levels, i.e., spiritually, esthetically and anthropologically.

John Muir said it best, "How many hearts with warm red blood in them are beating under cover of the woods, and how many teeth and eyes are shining? A multitude of animal people, intimately related to us, but whose lives we know almost nothing, are as busy about their own affairs as we are about ours."

Isn't it about time to read this book, become aware of their danger and take action to change human fecundity and population to come into balance with all of nature? Actually, we must take action before Mother Nature responds to our abuse. We enjoy a choice in 2021, but most certainly at some future date, we will lose that choice.

The seven ecological wounds

Dave Foreman pegs the "7 Deadly Sins" of overpopulation as they relate to the animal world. He exposes the human mob's onslaught of nature as a habitat killing machine.

That brings the moral-ethical question to the surface: does a cognitive species such as human beings possess the right to cause the extinction of countless other creatures? How many species can be sacrificed before nature cannot continue operating in balance with its ecosystems? Does humanity possess a responsibility to ensure survival of other species in the endless network of life on Earth?

To be certain, humanity stands at the gate of adding another 2.2 billion of its kind within 29 years by 2050. It could reach beyond 10 billion on its way to 14 billion as some demographers project.

With those numbers and ecological footprints exploding beyond imagination, Foreman addresses "The Seven Ecological Wounds" that humans slam onto the Natural World.

Wound 1: Overkill—Mankind has been killing wildlife since he migrated out of Africa. He shoots, traps, poisons, stomps and destroys habitat at lightning speed. He kills animals for feathers, adornments and sexual prowess.

Wound 2: Scalping and Taming Wilderness—He clears land for agriculture, logging, grazing, burning, killing keystone species, mining, dams, irrigation, oil spills and more. Humans wreck the land wherever they travel.

Wound 3: Fragmentation of Wildlife Neighborhoods— Since the Roman Empire, humans have methodically destroyed habitat with roads, canals, power lines and more.

Wound 4: Upsetting and Weakening Ecological and Evolutionary Processes—Humans destroy wildlife by predation, by knocking out pollinators, via hydrological disruption with dams and irrigation.

Wound 5: Spread of Exotic Species and Diseases—Man carries diseases, plants and vertebrates to new and unknown ecosystems that displace the native species.

Wound 6: Biocide Poisoning of Land, Air, Water and Wildlife—Humans have created farms, sewers, outhouses, mines, factories, oil tankers, toxic waste and much more in its destruction of the Natural World.

Wound 7: Global Weirding or Climate Change and Ocean Acidification—Air pollution and chemicals are destroying our lakes and oceans. Reefs and fish suffer under the onslaught of chemicals injected into the oceans.

While Americans, thus far, do not understand the consequences of overpopulation around the world, it races ahead at full speed. Somalia in October of 2011 received $100 million in food-aid to feed a million starving humans. However, to feed them means to grow their population until they die off in greater numbers in the future. At 1.3 billion people in 2021, Africa expects to grow to 4.1 billion by the end of this century.

Do you think the wild things of Africa stand a chance at such an onslaught of humans? (Source: United Nations "Populations Projections.")

Do you think that Africans stand a chance? Ecologist Marvin Harris said, "During the 1980's, some of the worst famines in history afflicted large parts of Africa and South Asia under the noses of the United Nations. In absolute numbers, more illiterate, impoverished and chronically malnourished people live in the world at the end of the 20th century than at the beginning."

Imagine an added 2.2 billion humans in less than 29 years romping around the planet for food! How about another 100 million added to America? Foreman slams reality into the face of anyone who thinks this is going to be a fun ride for our citizens.

Lester Brown, author of ***Plan B 4.0 Saving Civilization*** said, "The world has set in motion environmental trends that are threatening civilization itself. We are crossing environmental thresholds and violating deadlines set by nature. Nature is the timekeeper, but we cannot see the clock."

More Wise Words from Men of History

It's not like we haven't been warned about our fecundity. Herodotus over 2,000 years ago said, "Man stalks across the landscape, and deserts follow in his footsteps."

As you may know, desertification of the planet races forward at blinding speed.

Edward Abbey said, "Growth for the sake of growth is the ideology of a cancer cell."

Botanist Paul Sears said, "Man has become the sponsor of a biological experiment without known parallel in the history of the earth and its inhabitants. He has become the predominant species. He has destroyed the natural pattern and from the wreck is trying to create a new one. That is a cataclysmic revolution."

Foreman shows that humans race toward a very sobering future while they eradicate countless species.

As Foreman says, "The planet cannot afford more Americans."

He talks about the Jevons' Paradox. You must read it to grasp it.

Foreman brings a lifetime of compelling experiences to this book. Once you start it, you cannot put it down. It grabs you. It captivates your sense of responsibility. It compels you to take action.

Solutions to Solve the Human Dilemma of Overpopulation

After meeting Dave Foreman personally in Washington DC at a population conference, and after reading his book, I understand his deep caring about the extinction of the Natural World's wildlife.

Both of us love the wilds. We love Emerson, Thoreau, and John Muir. We loved Edward Abbey, Rachel Carson, Jane Goodall, Eleanor Roosevelt and Wallace Stegner for their brilliant connection to Mother Nature through their books.

Virginia Tech professor Eileen Crist said it compellingly, "It is critical to focus on what is presently dead certain: that overproduction and overpopulation have been driving the dismantling of complex ecosystems and native life, and leaving in their widening wake constructed environments (millions of folks in cities of concrete and toxic skies), lost ecologies and lost life forms."

From my own world travels and having trudged through the Amazon jungles, I witnessed what they wrote about. I watched the cutting and burning of the Amazon. I witnessed countless wildlife habitat acreage clear-cut and burned. Therefore, it's not something that I read about in a book. I watched it as it happened! It pained me and I felt helpless in the face of its savagery.

But when you look at Wall Street, whether in New York City

or in London, those dudes think only about "growth" of profits. They drive the bus of expansion, pillage and plunder. **Because the dollar rules all thought, they continue without anyone questioning or standing in their way.**

We must, as a species, get our leaders together, or we must gather ordinary citizens in whatever forums possible—and move the issue of human overpopulation into the forefront.

A country like the United Kingdom must question its sanity to grow by another 11 million within less than 20 years at its current immigration inflow. The UK represents a modern Easter Island. Such a pity the citizens of the UK don't see it…yet! But they most certainly will experience it in the coming years.

Second, help cut birthrates in overpopulated countries by sending birth control and family planning. Help them in their own countries.

Third, reform NAFTA, world trade and farm support to help hungry countries with hungry people.

Fourth, stop the ridiculous "War on Drugs" folly.

Fifth, coordinate to encourage two or preferably less children per woman worldwide. Optimum: one child per woman globally. This needs to happen, now!

Today, most world leaders ignore the population issue: even in the face of accelerating wars within and between nations. With 4.0 million children starving to death annually, isn't it about time to act with International Family Planning as the best method of choice to stop population overshoot?

Do you want to do something? Foreman offers a dozen pages of solutions and action websites. Join him and start your own in your own country. For all the retired folks in Europe,

Canada, America and Australia—become engaged for your grandkids' sake.

If you love wildlife, take action. Once you push the transmission into gear, more will join you. My father told me, "Son, if you believe in something, and you know you are right, you need to stand up and speak out. Especially against injustice or something you know is wrong. Because, when you do, you give courage, and you inspire 10,000 people behind you who are afraid to speak out for fear of some unknown reprisal."

SECTION 5

ODDS, ENDS AND SOLUTIONS

CHAPTER 32

//

HOW AND WHY JOURNALISTS AVOID THE POPULATION CONNECTION

"Mark Twain's famous 'silent assertion' [the big lie] lives, breathes and manifests in the 21ˢᵗ century. The press continues to obfuscate, cloud, deny, suppress and ignore America's and humanity's entire greatest dilemma: overpopulation." FHW

Why do you suppose most Americans remain apathetic to our hyper-population growth? What rational person supports water shortages, climate change, and worse ramifications caused by more people?

Surprise! Some vacant-minded folks don't see a problem. Several years ago, I personally called U.S. Congressman Chris Cannon, (R-UT). He said, "America can easily hold 1.0 billion people."

I nearly fell out of my chair. It's almost beyond my understanding that anyone can be that obtuse...another word for just plain stupid!

How do Americans live in denial? For the life of me, I don't understand.

The imminent writer T. Michael Maher said, "Recent surveys show that Americans are less concerned about population than they were 25 years ago, and they aren't connecting environmental degradation to population growth. Using a random sample of 150 stories about urban sprawl, endangered species and water shortages, this study shows that only about one story in ten framed population growth as a source of the problem."

Further, only one story in the entire sample mentioned population stability among the realm of possible solutions. Part II of the study presents the results of interviews with twenty-five journalists whose stories on local environmental problems omitted the causal role of population growth. It shows that journalists are aware of the controversial nature of the population issue, and prefer to avoid it if possible.

In 1992 the National Academy of Sciences and the British Royal Society issued a joint statement urging world leaders to brake population growth before it is too late. That same year, 1,600 scientists (including 99 Nobel laureates) issued a statement warning all humanity that it must soon stabilize population and halt environmental destruction. That same year, world leaders ignored population growth at the largest environmental summit in history, the U.N. Conference on Environment and Development, held in Rio de Janeiro.

"If present growth trends in population, industrialization, pollution, food production and resource depletion continue unchanged, the limits to growth will be reached sometime in the next 100 years." The Club of Rome 1972

The curiosity to me is, why are the American public and political leaders so indifferent about this issue that concerns the world's leading scientists and environmentalists? Our predicament worsens with every news cycle reporting on mounting environmental traumas, yet no connection. What's up with that?

Another recent Gallup Poll (Hueber, 1991), showed that 78 percent of Americans considered themselves environmentalists and 71 percent favored strong environmental protection, even at the expense of economic growth. How can Americans express strong concern about the environment, yet a diminishing concern about population growth, which many environmental experts consider the ultimate environmental problem?

Do you see the disconnect from reality based on our history of unlimited resources, land, water and air? We continue with the myth of limitless expansion via entitlement. If we ignore it, like a child that places his/her hands over its eyes, the bad thing vanishes. If we ignore the 'monster' called 'too many people', since it's not harming us today, it can be discounted.

Population researchers Paul and Anne Ehrlich opened their book,

The Population Explosion, with a chapter titled, "Why Isn't Everyone as Scared as We Are?"

Ehrlich acknowledged, "The average person, even the average scientist, seldom makes the connection between environmental problems and the population problem, and thus remains unworried."

But while they noted that the evening news almost never connects population growth to environmental problems, the Ehrlich's chiefly blamed social taboos fostered by the Catholic Church and 'a colossal failure of education' for public indifference about population.

How Experts Frame Environmental Causality

This vital information gets lost in the media shuffle: with specific reference to habitat loss, Sears (1956), Jackson (1981), Myers (1991), Ehrlich and Ehrlich (1990), Harrison (1992) and many others, have shown that population growth pushes people into relatively pristine, natural environments. Endangered species problems are frequently the flip side of this coin: when people convert wildlife habitat to their own habitat, they bulldoze trees, introduce chemicals, divert streams, build dams, alter the water table, and disrupt habitat in numerous other ways.

While it is well known that environmental experts connect environmental degradation to population growth, it is less well known that land developers are equally straightforward in implicating population growth as a causal agent for turning wildlife habitat and farmland into subdivisions.

Maher said, "The search produced 1,349 water shortage stories, 1,942 urban sprawl stories, and 6,001 endangered species stories. To be considered for coding, the story had to describe a population-driven environmental conflict."

Of the 150 article sample, 16 (less than 11 percent) mentioned population growth as a cause of the environmental problem described in the story. Population growth appeared in eight urban sprawl stories, seven water shortage stories, and one story on endangered species.

Although many scientific groups, environmental scientists and even land development experts agree that population growth is a basic cause of environmental change, media framing diverges widely from expert framing.

Just over 10 percent of a Lexis-Nexis sample of environmental news stories links human population growth to the environmental problems it affects.

It's ironic, but only one story in a sample of 150 presents the view that limiting population growth might be a solution to environmental problems. Such stories tell the reader: population growth affects environmental degradation, but population stability is too unimportant to be mentioned as a policy option.

Ignoring that a stable population might be a long-term solution to environmental problems, news stories instead direct the public's attention to palliative solutions: build new dams to supply water, zone to prevent urban sprawl, set aside land for endangered species. In my State of Colorado, the governor built more dams, created more light-rail and built more lanes on Interstate twenty-five. Those actions, in fact, caused more growth rather than alleviate the problem. Result: demographers predict Colorado to add 5.0 million by mid-century.

"In thousands of communities across America, population growth wreaks changes: a mobile home park displaces an orchard, a farmer loses his water rights to a city hundreds of miles away, an endangered reptile's last known habitat is threatened by a subdivision," Maher said. "These and countless other population-influenced disruptions reduce wildlife habitat, rural solitude, water availability, and many other environmental qualities."

But this study shows that only one news story in ten connects these events to population growth.

In plain English, those writers entrusted with informing the American public, pass the buck, which verifies the genius of Mark Twain's "silent assertion." Again, those writers sustain Einstein's adage when he said, "There are two things infinite: the universe and human stupidity."

CHAPTER 33

//

OUR UNINFORMED AND UNWILLING LEADERS

"Cautious, careful people, always casting about to preserve their reputation and social standing. They can never bring about reform. Those who are really in earnest must be willing to be anything or nothing in the world's estimation, and publicly and privately, in season and out, avow their sympathy with despised and persecuted ideas and their advocates, and bear the consequences." Susan B. Anthony, women's suffrage

As you read through this information, you may discover a new level of education, awareness and intellectual sobriety. We as a species and as a civilization stand at the edge of the abyss.

Astoundingly enough, our world and national leaders look into human overpopulation with intrepid stupidity. Our church leaders cannot bring themselves out of their religious stupors long enough to face facts. Regular citizens stand in denial or awake completely clueless each day.

As long as we cannot experience what we see on television around the world, it's easy to live in denial or refutation of our accelerating dilemma.

For example, everyone watched what happened to New Orleans during Hurricane Katrina, while 99 percent of Americans did not experience it nor its current ongoing aftermath years later. The horror of 9/11 affected 3,000 people and several thousand loved ones—with death. The clean-up crews agonized through it, but for the most part, the country didn't lose much sleep over the World Trade Towers collapsing.

Let's revisit Eleanor Roosevelt's wise words: **"We must prevent human**

tragedy rather than run around trying to save ourselves after an event has already occurred. Unfortunately, history clearly shows that we arrive at catastrophe by failing to meet the situation, by failing to act when we should have acted. The opportunity passes us by, and the next disaster is always more difficult and compounded than the last one."

Do you see any national or world leaders addressing overpopulation? Which U.S. governors address it? Any U.S. Senators? Have any leaders offered solutions? The harsh answer: no!

Yes, you hear about Al Gore's crusade concerning climate change. Sweden's Greta Thunberg urges all countries and adults to take action. America's Adam Roberti, a youth with abundant enthusiasm, speaks and writes to encourage all generations to take action. I've been speaking and writing about it for 30 years. However, notice that Gore and Thunberg fail to mention population stabilization as a remedy when population increases directly accelerate climate change.

You watch church organizations like "Save the Children" show horrific video projections of millions of starving children in Africa and other parts of the world. They invite you to send money to save starving children.

But, they won't provide birth control. That means the more children they save beget millions more that will starve at a later date. You may see the Pope pray for food and assistance for starving masses, but he won't advocate for birth control. He preaches against it. You see our presidents advocating for more oil drilling, but not for conservation.

Everything you've read in this book occurs in greater degrees daily as the world population grows by 83 million annually. It's not getting better; it's becoming much worse.

So Why Do Our Leaders Fail Us?

They fail because we fail to elect visionary leaders. We respond to emotions rather than conditions. We await this "Human Katrina" rather than work to circumvent it.

They and we fail because our culture expects unlimited and unending access to expansion, growth and resources—The American Dream.

Ruthless capitalism pleases many in the short term, but decimates our planet in the long term.

They and we fail because not enough people understand what you're learning by reading this book.

CHAPTER 34

///

CATASTROPHIC CLIMATE DESTABILIZATION'S MARKERS

"Adults keep saying we owe it to the young people, to give them hope, but I don't want your hope. I don't want you to be hopeful. I want you to panic. I want you to feel the fear I feel every day. I want you to act. I want you to act as you would in a crisis. I want you to act as if your house is on fire, because it is."

Greta Thunberg, 17 year-old Swedish Activist

Each one of these news reports indicates our climate heating up. You will see more and more of them in the coming years.

1. Lewistown, Montana, (70 degrees Fahrenheit) and Klamath Falls, Oregon, (65 degrees) set high-temperature records for the month of February 2020.
3. California had its driest February on record, 2020.
4. In April 2020, parts of southern Arizona and California saw the mercury climb past 100 degrees Fahrenheit for multiple days in a row, shattering records.
5. Nome, Alaska, experienced its warmest May 2020 since record-keeping began in the early 1900's.
6. Seven large fires burned across more than 75,000 acres in Arizona during May 2020, and in early June. Lightning ignited the Bighorn Fire in the Santa Catalina Mountains near Tucson, ultimately torching 120,000 acres. A week later, the Bush Fire broke out in Maricopa County and became the fifth largest in the state's history.

7. On July 10, 2020, Alamosa, Colorado, set a temperature record for a daily low (37 degrees Fahrenheit). Later that day, it set another record for the daily high (92 degrees).

8. Phoenix, Arizona, set an all-time record for monthly mean temperature in July, (98.3 degrees), only to see that record fall in August (99.1 degrees Fahrenheit). The temperature in the burgeoning city exceeded 100 degrees on 145 days in 2020 — another record.

9. In the Western region in August 2020, 214 monthly and 18 all-time high-temperature records were tied or broken, including in Porthill, Idaho (103 degrees), Mazama, Washington (103 degrees) and Goodwin Peak, Oregon (101 degrees).

10. By the end of October 2020, Phoenix had experienced 197 heat-associated deaths — about five times the yearly average during the early 2000's.

11. In Death Valley National Park, the mercury hit 130 on August 16, 2020, breaking the previous all-time record set in 2013.

12. Across the Western U.S., hundreds of monthly and all-time high-temperature records were broken in August 2020, including in several places in Idaho and Washington, where the mercury climbed above 100 degrees.

13. Warm temperatures in Alaska caused ice on the Chukchi Sea to melt, leaving record-tying amounts of open sea.

14. During monsoon season (June through August), Phoenix received just 1.0 inch of rain, or about 37 percent of average, and then received no precipitation at all in September or October 2020.

15. Grand Junction, Colorado, experienced its driest July and August on record. On July 31, 2020, lightning ignited the nearby Pine Gulch Fire, which grew to 139,000 acres, making it (briefly) the largest in state history, only to be eclipsed by the 207,000 acre Cameron Peak Fire in the northern part of the state. (I live in the woods at 8,000 feet near Evergreen, Colorado, so I can assure you we were all sweating bullets.)

16. Colorado's wildfire season was not only its most severe on record, but most of the fires also burned far later in the year than normal. In mid-October, when Colorado's mountains would normally be covered with snow, the East Troublesome Fire west of Boulder tore through

high-elevation forests and homes to become the state's second-largest fire ever. Shortly thereafter, the Ice Fire broke out at nearly 10,000 feet above sea level in what was once known as the "asbestos forest" near Silverton, burning over 500 acres.

17. A dry thunderstorm that generated more than 8,000 recorded lightning strikes hit Central and Northern California in late July 2020, igniting multiple megafires. The resulting August Complex became the largest fire in state history, and together with the SCU Lightning Complex, the LNU Lightning Complex and the North Complex fires, it burned across more than two-million acres, destroyed 5,000 structures and killed 22 people.

18. Smoke from California's fires spread across the region, causing particulate matter to build up to levels that were hazardous to health and significantly diminishing solar energy output.

19. In September 2020, several fires were sparked in Oregon's tinder-dry forests. Fueled by high winds, they went on to burn more than one-million acres and 4,000 homes.

20. In August the Rio Grande in New Mexico shrank to the lowest mean monthly flow since 1973. Other rivers in the region, including the Colorado, Green and San Juan, ran at far-below-average levels throughout the summer.

21. As of early November 2020, Lake Powell's surface elevation had declined by 35 feet since the same date in 2017, and summer hydroelectric output from Glen Canyon Dam's turbines was 13 percent below the previous summer's. (26)

CHAPTER 35

//

NEW DIRECTION FOR HUMAN POPULATION

"Already the once sweet-watered streams, most of which bore Indian names, were clouded with silt and the wastes of man; the very earth was being ravaged and squandered. To the Indians it seemed that these Europeans hated everything in nature—the living forests and their birds and beasts, the grassy glades, the water, the soil, and the air itself." Dee Brown, Bury My Heart at Wounded Knee

"This planet ain't big enough for 7,800,000,000 humans," said Chris Rapley of the Belfast Telegraph in the United Kingdom.

Again, if you visit (www.populationmedia.org) or (www.worldpopulationbalance.org), you may see how fast human numbers explode across the planet on a minute-by-minute basis. It's pretty unnerving to see it in front of your eyes. For me, it's beyond unnerving because I've seen the human debris of those numbers on my world bicycle travels. The human race stands up to its eyebrows in trouble.

"Behind the climate crisis lurks a global issue that no one wants to tackle: we need radical plans to reduce the world's population," Rapley said. "What do the following have in common: the carbon dioxide content of the atmosphere, Earth's average temperature and the size of the human population?"

Answer: each was, for a long period of Earth's history, held in a state of equilibrium. Whether it's the burning of fossil fuels versus the rate at which plants absorb carbon, or the heat absorbed from sunshine versus the heat reflected back into space, or global birth rates versus death rates—each is governed by the difference between an inflow and an outflow, and even small imbalances can have large outcomes. At present, all of these three are out of balance as a result of human actions. And each of these imbalances is creating a major problem.

Rapley continued, "Second question: how do these three differ? Answer: human carbon emissions and climate change are big issues at the top of the news agenda. And rightly so, since they pose a substantial threat. But population growth is almost entirely ignored. Which is odd, since it is at the root of the environmental crisis."

The statistics are quite alarming. For most of the two million years of human history, the population was less than a quarter of a million. The advent of agriculture led to a sustained increase, but it took thousands of years, until 1800, before the planet was host to a billion humans. Since then, growth has accelerated. We hit 2.0 in 1930, 3.0 billion in 1960, 4.0 billion in 1975, 5.0 billion in 1987 and 6.0 billion in 1999. Today's grand total stands at 7.8 billion.

"To what can we attribute such a dramatic rise?" asked Rapley. "Impressive increases in the food supply have played a part, but the underlying driver has been the shift from an "organic" society, in which energy was drawn from the wind, water, beasts of burden and wood, to a fossil fuel-based world in which most of our energy is obtained by burning coal, oil and gas. Although unevenly distributed, these bounties have seen life expectancy double and a corresponding reduction in mortality rates."

But success in reducing mortality has not been matched by a lowering of the birth rate—and this has resulted in the dramatic increase in the human stock. As noted by Malthus, who at the end of the 18th century was the first to foresee the problems of population growth, such growth can accelerate rapidly since every individual has the capacity to produce many offspring, each of whom can in turn produce many more, and the process will only cease when something happens to bring birth rate and death rate once more into balance.

"In fact, the overall growth rate of the world's population hit a peak of about two per cent per year in the late sixties and has since fallen to 1.3 percent," said Rapley. "Although the timing and magnitude of the changes have been different in various parts of the world, the pattern has followed the so-called 'demographic transition'. Initially both mortality and birth rates are high, with the population stable. The resulting difference between the numbers of births and deaths causes the population to increase. Eventually, the birth rate decreases until a new balance is achieved and the population again stabilizes, but at a new and higher level."

Demographers offer two possible explanations for the decline in birth rate, suggesting that it is an inherent tendency of societies to find equilibrium between births and deaths, with the lag simply being the time taken for the change in mortality rate to be recognized.

Alternatively, it is attributed to the same general driving forces that caused the decline in mortality, such as improvements in medical practice and technology, in this case birth control.

So where do we stand today? Worldwide, the birth rate is about "six per second," and the death rate stands at "three per second."

United Nations figures foresee numbers leveling out at a point when humans reach between nine and 10 billion by 2050.

Even at current levels, the World Health Organization reports that more than three billion people are malnourished as of 2020. And although food availability continues to grow, per capita grain availability has been declining since the eighties. Technology may continue to push back the limits, but 50 percent of plants and animals are already harvested for our use, creating a huge impact on our partner species and the world's ecosystems. And it is the airborne waste from our energy production that is driving climate change.

Yet, even at a geo-political level, population control is rarely discussed. In 2020, however, the publication of a new report on population made by the United Nations Environment Program might be the spur we need.

If debate commences, some will say that we need to stop the world's population from booming, and to do so most urgently where the birth rates are highest in the developing world. Others may argue that it is in the developed world, where the impact of individuals is highest, that we should concentrate efforts. A third view is to ignore population and to focus on human consumption.

Programs that seek to reduce birth rates find that three conditions must be met. First, birth control must be within the scope of conscious choice. Second, there must be real advantages to having a smaller family— if no provision is made for peoples' old age; the incentive is to have more children. Third, the means of control must be available—but also to be socially acceptable, and combined with education and emancipation of girls and women.

The human multitude has become a force on a planetary scale. Collectively, our exploitation of the world's resources has already reached a level that, according to the World Wildlife Fund, could only be sustained on a planet 25 per cent larger than our own.

But by avoiding a fraction of the projected population increase, the emissions savings could be significant and would be at a cost, based on UN experience of reproductive health programs, that would be as little as one-thousandth of the technological fixes. The reality is that while the footprint of each individual cannot be reduced to zero, the absence of an individual does do so.

"Although I'm now the director of the British Antarctic Survey," said Rapley. "I was previously executive director of the International Geosphere-Biosphere program, looking at the chemistry and biology of how Earth works as a system. About 18 months ago, I wrote an article for the BBC Green Room website in which I raised the issues: "So if we believe that the size of the human footprint is a serious problem, then a rational view would be that along with a raft of measures to reduce the footprint per person, the issue of population management must be addressed."

In practice, of course, it is a bombshell of a topic, with profound and emotive issues of ethics, morality, equity and practicability. So controversial is the subject that it has become the Cinderella of the great sustainability debate—rarely visible in public, or even in private. In interdisciplinary meetings addressing how the planet functions as an integrated whole, demographers and population specialists are usually notable by their absence. Rare, indeed, are the opportunities for religious leaders, philosophers, moralists, policy-makers, politicians and the global public to debate the trajectory of the world's human population in the context of its stress on the Earth system, and to decide what might be done.

"The response from around the world was strong and positive—along the lines of 'at last, this issue has been raised'," said Rapley. "But after that initial burst of enthusiasm, I find that little has changed. This is a pity, since as time passes, so our ability to leave the world in a better state is reduced. For the sake of future generations, I hope that others will this time take up the challenge."

How can an international journalist like Chris Rapley write about our human dilemma while our national leaders avoid it? If our leaders continue failing to raise this issue into the national and international spotlight, we face definite consequences as related by famous biologist Garrett Hardin.

Garrett Hardin's Three Laws Of Human Ecology

Garrett Hardin presented these three laws of human ecology, which are fundamental, and need to be known and recognized by all that would speak of sustainability.
(Source: www.GarrettHardinSociety.org)

First Law: We can never do merely one thing.

In other words, we are all woven into the web of life. I quote from one of my favorite authors, John Muir who said, "When you pick up a rock, you realize it's hitched to the universe."

Second Law: There's no 'away' to throw to.

This law illustrates that when a person 'throws something away', it goes somewhere. That means acid rain, chemicals, trash and pollution of any kind will affect something else in this limited biosphere.

Third Law: The impact (I) of any group or nation on the environment is represented qualitatively by the equation:

$$I = P\,A\,T$$

Here P is the size of the population, A is the per-capita affluence, measured by per-capita annual consumption, and T is a measure of the damage done by the technologies that are used in supplying the consumption. Hardin attributes this law to Ehrlich and Holdren. (Source: Ehrlich and Holdren 1971)

As revealed countless times in this book, we continue to continue ignoring the obvious that America is horrendously overpopulated—at our peril. My best guess? The United States will stagger along the same path as China, India, Bangladesh, Mexico, Africa and the rest of those overpopulated countries until our misery exceeds our ability to continue adding population.

Unfortunately, by that time, it will not be pretty. In fact, extreme ugliness awaits us.

CHAPTER 36

//

QUALITY OF LIFE

"Whether we accept it or not, this will likely be the century that determines what the optimal human population is for our planet. It will come about in one of two ways: Either we decide to manage our own numbers, to avoid a collision of every line on civilization's graph-or nature will do it for us, in the form of famines, thirst, climate chaos, crashing ecosystems, opportunistic disease, and wars over dwindling resources that finally cut us down to size." Alan Weisman, Countdown: Our Last Best Hope for a Future on Earth?

Thomas Jefferson proposed that every American enjoy, "Life, liberty and the pursuit of happiness." In 1776, that meant food, shelter, a rich and rewarding family-life, spiritual awakening, employment and creative expression.

High-speed, high-stress life—is that what you want?

In the 21st century, another phrase becomes more important in our high speed—high stress lives. *Quality of life* surfaced in the American lexicon in the last twenty years. Why? Because we grew too much, moved too fast and suffered accelerating consequences.

For those of you who experienced the 1950's and 60's, no one ever heard about gridlocked traffic, air pollution, species extinction, global warming, zip codes, overpopulation, cell phones, computers or drugs. Most guys knew every make, model and year of our cars.

Choices included Chevy, Plymouth, Ford, Chrysler and some strange little Japanese import called a Datsun.

In 1965, Elvis Presley drove Cadillac convertibles while John Wayne assured us that the 'good guys' always wore white hats. Jimmy Durante clowned on TV while Frank Sinatra crooned in Vegas. Los Angeles enjoyed Sunset Strip, Route 66 and Hollywood. California sported 16 million people.

What we face!

Fifty-six years later, California sports 39 million high stressed, high speed, road-raging and smart-phone-talking citizens. They endure gridlocked traffic, 1.5 hour commutes, air-polluted and gang-infested towns and cities. That's for starters! California expects an added 15 to 20 million people by 2050.

Would anyone say that the quality of life in Los Angeles, San Francisco, Chicago, Atlanta, New York City, Detroit, Miami, Houston, and our nation's capital— or any other multiple million populated city— measures up to something envisioned by our founders as reasonable and appropriate?

In 2010, I spent four days in Washington, DC at the annual Federation for American Immigration Reform *"Hold Their Feet to the Fire"* conference where 35 national radio hosts and hundreds of their esteemed guests spoke to millions of listeners concerning unchecked immigration. If I could hang a literary handle on the East Coast, I'd say, "too many people, too many cars, too much noise, too much pollution, too many accidents, unbelievably gridlocked traffic and stinky"— just for starters! (www. Fairus.org)

In truth, DC took my breath away

I am astounded that people hit the expressways at 4:30 a.m., daily, to beat the rush hour. I jumped on the Metro Subway at Shady Grove 30 miles out of Washington, DC. By the time I reached Union Station, I felt like a sardine crammed into a tin.

Unpleasant, unhealthy, obnoxious and insufferable! As I stepped off the subway, old ladies tried to run over me on their rush to the escalator.

I felt like a cork being swept away in a human ocean of people. Every metropolitan arena featured maddening crowds and endless congestion.

The traffic within and around our cities grows to crisis gridlocked levels. What's the latest plan to alleviate the beltways around our cities? Engineers plan to build second beltways around the first beltways— some are already completed!

The future will bring more overcrowding, unless

Where does hyper-population growth lead us? What about quality of life? What about peace of mind? First, a reminder— with thanks to Webster's Dictionary:

> Overpopulation is the condition of any organism's numbers exceeding the carrying capacity of its ecological niche. In common parlance, the term usually refers to the relationship between the human population and its environment, the Earth.
>
> Overpopulation is not simply a function of the size or density of the population, but rather the number of individuals compared to the resources (for example, food production or water resources) and 'personal space' needed for healthy survival or well-being.

Are these simple examples good things?

Stop for a moment and close your eyes as you consider our current dilemma. Have you noticed the little advantages we lose as we overpopulate?

- You must dial all 10 digits for local phone calls today because of our massive population overload in our cities— some regions feature five area codes.
- Commuters added 20 to 30 minutes to commute time in the past 15 years. They can expect to add another 20 minutes in the coming 10 years. It's not uncommon in many states for 1.5 hour commute times.
- In some regions you are already expected to make reservations by lottery for our national parks— within 20 years, we will all be

doing that because too many people want to visit those limited spaces.

- You can't beg, borrow or buy a campsite in places like Yosemite National Park because endless millions of people beat you to it.
- As highways overload with another 100 million people, your chances of making it to and from your destination erode dramatically— with more risk. Currently, 40,000 people die from traffic accidents every year, and tens of thousands suffer injuries to one degree or another in "accidents." Those numbers grow exponentially as we add 100 million people.
- The "quality-time" that nourishes each of us diminishes; we suffer that loss.
- Family doctors report that 75 percent of diagnoses are stress related.
- Your water, electrical and property taxes will rise with the rise in demand for natural resources and the production of energy.
- Expect your food bills to rise dramatically as demand accelerates.

You can enumerate another 50 examples of the loss of quality of life from your neck of the woods. Do you want to bequeath this situation to your children?

Change Can Be Managed, And Strategies Chosen Sensibly

Understanding our loss of quality of life:

In the context of human societies, overpopulation occurs when the population density becomes so great as to actually cause an impaired quality of life, serious environmental degradation, and/or long-term shortages of essential goods and services.

Overpopulation is not merely an imbalance between the number of individuals compared to the resources needed for survival, or a ratio of population over resources, or a function of the number or density of individuals, compared to the resources (i.e., food production) they need to survive.

It is rather a situation of shortage of resources and space that must be caused by population, and not by other factors. Such an imbalance may be caused by any number of other factors including bad governance, war, corruption or endemic poverty.

People feel each human-crowding factor as an agitation, a gnawing and bothersome affect that is difficult to describe— until you venture into a pristine natural area, and begin breathing deeply. Then, you remember what you really enjoy. And don't!

Please ask yourself; why choose to drift aimlessly into this overcrowding? America invites its hyper-population growth by absorbing millions of immigrants annually. (28)

Strategic Action and Planning Work!

It may startle you to learn a basic truth; those nations already manifest what we move toward: China, Indonesia, Mexico, India, Egypt, much of Africa, Bangladesh, Pakistan and so many more. They failed to plan for population balancing, and neither do we.

What are we thinking? In this fragile Republic of the United States, we participate in a grand experiment. Until recently, the ride proved fun. Of late, the elbow room to play diminishes—along with our creative-competitive energies.

How will you turn the horses and halt our unchecked population growth? Is your 'peace-of-mind' and optimized quality-of-life worth the effort? Do you owe that healthy legacy to your children?

Quality-of-life; one day you enjoy it and the next, it's gone.

CHAPTER 37

///

HEADLINES OF OUR TIMES

"Many days we shake our heads because the news is so bad, we ignore it, and for some reason, we go on living and don't think much about it. However, that won't work for our children's outlook. We must take action in order to change the present and the future. This is a matter of integrity and personal responsibility." FHW

Perhaps, after reading this book, you wish you didn't know what you know right now! You might be distressed or angry. You may feel hopeless. You might think everything in this book cannot be happening or that it's all conjecture on the part of the author. In fact, as you see from many of the dates back as far as 2000, the human race added another 1.5 billion people, which means the damages multiplied further.

I researched far and wide for news stories from around the country and planet that directly validate in a variety of ways what I have written and what I have witnessed in my world travels.

The following journalists report the facts that impact every human, plant and animal in our country and on this planet.

Again, as our numbers accelerate, everything you read in this chapter worsens all over the globe. We either stop the abuse of our planet home, or it will stop us.

News Headlines That Cannot Be Ignored—Hold on To Your Hat

Who would have predicted a century ago that the richest civilization in history would be made up of polluted tracts of suburban development dominated by the private automobile, shopping malls, and a throwaway economy? Surely, this is not the ultimate fulfillment of our destiny.

Alan Durning, **How Much Is Enough?** 1992

Over 24 years, the government and private research agencies dumped almost 48,000 55 gallon drums of radioactive waste just a few miles west of the Golden Gate Bridge. That waste now is leaking into the Gulf of the Farallon National Marine Sanctuary—and no one knows how much contamination it is causing in seafood. Most are so corroded that moving them would spread more radioactive waste. It was dumped between 1946 and 1970 at what then was called the Farallon Islands Nuclear Waste Site.

Colleen Valles, "Bay Area May Be in Hot Water Over Dumping,"
LA Times.com, February 17, 2002

The safe disposal of sewage sludge is an enormous task. American sewage treatment plants produce 11.6 billion pounds of sewage sludge each year. More than a third is spread on farmland or otherwise mixed into soils. In addition to being "human manure," sewage sludge can contain toxic chemicals, heavy metals and pathogens.

Michael Vatalaro, *"EPA Intimidates Sludge Critics, Congress Told"*
Environmental News Service March 22, 2000

A dense blanket of pollution, dubbed the "Asian Brown Cloud," is hovering over South Asia, with scientists warning it could kill millions of people in the region, and pose a global threat. In the biggest-ever study of the phenomenon, 200 scientists warned that the cloud, estimated to be two miles thick, is responsible for hundreds of thousands of deaths a year from respiratory disease. The potent haze lying over the entire Indian subcontinent—from Sri Lanka to Afghanistan—has led to some erratic weather, sparking flooding in Bangladesh, Nepal and northeastern India, but drought in Pakistan and northwestern India.

Marianne Bray, "Asian Brown Cloud poses global threat"
CNN.com August 12, 2002

Every one of you sitting here today is carrying at least 500 measurable chemicals in your body that were never in anybody's body before the 1920's. We have dusted the globe with man-made chemicals that can undermine the development of the brain and behavior, and the endocrine, immune and reproductive systems, vital systems that assure perpetuity. You are not exposed to one chemical at a time, but a complex mixture of chemicals that changes day by day, hour by hour, depending on where you are and the environment you are in. In the United States alone, it is estimated that over 84,000 different chemicals are used regularly.

Theo Colburn, *"Speech at the State of the World Forum"*
San Francisco, October 3, 1996

Without requiring lab tests to determine their safety, the U.S. government has approved thousands of chemicals for use in such products as sofa cushions, soaps, paints and baby bottles. On average, two more chemicals are approved every day. The result: Consumers are unwittingly part of a vast, uncontrolled lab experiment. "We're treating people worse than lab rats," said Karen Florini, a lawyer with the nonprofit group Environmental Defense.

Tom Avril, *"U.S. chemical regulation leaves much unknown"*
Philadelphia Inquirer, November 4, 2003

More than eight million pounds of persistent toxic metals (like lead and mercury) were released into our waterways (in 1997), an increase of more than 50 percent from the previous year and the largest amount since at least 1992. Nearly 900,000 pounds of reproductive toxins like toluene were released into U.S. waterways, an increase of 60 percent from the previous year and the largest amount released since at least 1992. The parent corporations with the greatest amounts of toxic pollution to waterways were Armco Inc., PCS Nitrogen Fertilizer LP, BASF Corporation, E. I. Du Pont De Nemours & Co., and Vicksburg Chemical Co.

Cat Lazaroff, *"Polluters Sully US Waters Despite Federal Regulations"*
Environment News Service, February 17, 2000

By the time the Raccoon River winds through the hills in western Iowa, passing corn fields and livestock pens before reaching Des Moines, it is so polluted the city has to put it through a special nutrient filter to meet government standards for drinking water. Across the country, metropolitan water agencies are battling increasing pollution from the countryside. The river pollution is spreading and helping to cause dead zones in the open seas. A recent study by the Pew Oceans Commission, an independent group examining government policies, called huge livestock feedlots and farm fertilizer runoff among the fastest-growing sources of pollution in oceans thousands of miles away.

Elizabeth Becker, *"Big farms making a mess of U.S. Waters"*
The New York Times, February 10, 2002

Hundreds of millions of tiny plastic pellets, or nurdles—the raw materials for the plastic industry—are lost or spilled every year, working their way into the sea. These pollutants act as chemical sponges attracting man-made chemicals such as hydrocarbons and the pesticide DDT. They then enter the food chain. "What goes into the ocean goes into these animals and onto your dinner plate. It's that simple," said Dr Eriksen.

Kathy Marks & Daniel Howden, *"The World's Dump"*
The Independent UK, February 6, 2008

Dust and soot in the air contribute to between 20 and 200 early deaths each day in America's biggest cities, according to the largest coast-to-coast scientific study of the problem. Ill health from particulates, tiny specks smaller than the width of a human hair, is spread across 20 of the largest cities in the United States—including Los Angeles, Santa Ana-Anaheim,

San Bernardino and three other California areas—which are inhabited by about 10 million people. The researchers found strong evidence that dust and soot particles, not other factors suggested by industry, appear to be causing the harmful effects.

Gary Polakovic, *"Study Links Deaths to Airborne Particles"*
Los Angeles Times, December 14, 2000

Between November of 1999 and December of 2000, EPA filed lawsuits against nine power companies for expanding their plants without obtaining New Source Review permits and the up-to-date pollution controls required by law. The companies named in our lawsuits emit an incredible 5 million tons of sulfur dioxide every year as well as 2 million tons of nitrogen oxide. Data supplied to the Senate Environmental Committee by EPA last year, estimated the annual health bill from 7 million tons of SO2 and NO2: more than 10,800 premature deaths; at least 5,400 incidents of chronic bronchitis; more than 5,100 hospital emergency visits; and over 1.5 million lost workdays. Add to that severe damage to our natural resources, as acid rain attacks soils and plants and deposits nitrogen in the Chesapeake Bay and other critical bodies of water.

Eric V. Schaeffer, Director of U.S. Environmental Protection Agency's Office of Regulatory Enforcement, Resignation Letter, February 27, 2002

The Environmental Protection Agency believes that about 630,000 of the roughly four million babies born annually in the United States — twice as many as previously thought — may be exposed to dangerous levels of mercury in the womb, according to an analysis released Thursday. The primary source of newborns' exposure to mercury is the fish and shellfish their mothers eat. Mercury in children can impair motor functions, learning capacity, vision and memory, and can cause a variety of other symptoms related to neurological damage.

Elizabeth Shogren, *"Estimate of Fetuses Exposed to High*
Mercury Doubles" LA Times.com, February 6, 2004

We are told that we cannot afford clean air and water and health for our children. Yet in the first few months of 2001, you and I spent over $2 billion buying videos. Brides-to-be will spend over $35 billion on weddings this year, and Americans will spend a staggering $550 billion on gambling. Corporations will spend untold billions on advertising.

Jackie Alan Giuliano, *"Earth Day 2001-A Celebration or a Wake?"*
Environmental News Service, April 20, 2001

America's cities, blanketed with smog and climate-altering carbon dioxide, have become cradles of ill health and are fostering an epidemic of asthma, according to a report yesterday from a leading group of Harvard University researchers and the American Public Health Association. Particularly hard hit are preschool-aged children, whose rate of asthma rose by 160 percent between 1980 and 1994 (more than twice the national average). As well, particulates—or small bits—from burned diesel fuel attach themselves to mold and pollen, which in turn is delivered deep into human lung sacs. A measure of the impact is that a quarter of the children living in Harlem are asthmatic, and they are concentrated along bus routes, the researchers said.

Alanna Mitchell, *"Global warming linked to high asthma rates"*
The Globe and Mail, April 30, 2004

The dead zone this summer reached 8,500 square miles, about as big as Massachusetts, to become the largest mass of oxygen-starved water ever recorded in the Gulf of Mexico. Crab carcasses lie covered in a bacterial mat as if spray painted white. In pockets where oxygen is totally depleted, the surface may appear clear, if a bit too glassy, while bottom waters faintly smell of rotten eggs. "Call it the Berlin Wall of the gulf," said former Louisiana shrimper Donald Lirette, "because life can't cross it from either side."

Rick Montgomery, Knight Ridder News Service,
"Sea suffocates in 'dead zone" St. Paul Pioneer Press, October 29, 2002

A first-of-its-kind study of Iowa's 132 lakes shows they are among the most fertilizer-polluted waters on Earth. "We suspected Iowa has some of the most nutrient-rich water in the world, and this proves it," Iowa State University researcher John Downing said Monday. Downing's conclusion is based on three rounds of samples from each of Iowa's 132 lakes, all taken last summer. The samples show heavy concentrations of nitrates and phosphorus, two common ingredients in farm and yard runoff.

Perry Beeman, *"Iowa's lakes among filthiest in the world"*
The Des Moines Register, March 6, 2001

For nearly 40 years, while producing the now-banned industrial coolants known as PCB's at a local factory, Monsanto Company routinely discharged toxic waste into a west Anniston creek [Alabama] and dumped millions of pounds of PCB's into oozing open-pit landfills. And thousands of pages of Monsanto documents—many emblazoned with warnings such as "CONFIDENTIAL: Read and Destroy" –show that for decades; the corporate giant concealed what it did and what it knew. In 1966, Monsanto managers discovered that fish submerged in that creek turned belly-up within 10 seconds, spurting blood and shedding skin as if dunked into boiling water. In 1969, they found fish in another creek with 7,500 times the legal PCB levels. They ordered its conclusion changed from "slightly tumorigenic" to "does not appear to be carcinogenic."

Michael Grunwald, *"Monsanto Hid Decades of Pollution"*
Washington Post, January 1, 2002

During those years, St. Louis-based Monsanto flushed tens of thousands of pounds of PCB's and other toxic wastes into Snow Creek each year. More than 45 tons of PCB's, a highly efficient industrial insulator, were discharged in 1969 alone. Monsanto also deposited millions of pounds of PCB's in a hillside landfill just above the plant.

"This is by far the most contaminated community, as indicated by the levels in their blood, that I've ever encountered," Dr. Nisbet said.

"We would all rather live in a pristine world," said Jere White, a lawyer for Monsanto and Solutia, in his opening argument two weeks ago. "We are all going to be exposed to things on a daily basis. Our bodies can deal with it."

Kevin Sack, "*PCB pollution suits have day in court in Alabama*"

New York Times, January 27, 2002

A chemical widely found in food packaging and other plastics may cause severe genetic defects in embryos, at levels people are commonly exposed to, according to a scientific study published today. Laboratory experiments by geneticists at Case Western Reserve University in Ohio showed that bisphenol 'A' disrupts the way that chromosomes align to produce the eggs of mice, leading to aneuploidy, which is the main cause of miscarriages and Down's syndrome in humans. Scientists say the study is the first to show that exposure to a small amount of an environmental contaminant that mimics the hormone estrogen disrupts the growth of embryos, killing them or leading to genetically abnormal offspring.

Marla Cone, "*Study Links Plastics to Embryo Ills*"
Los Angeles Times, April 1, 2003

The Environmental Protection Agency concluded yesterday that long-term exposure to exhaust from diesel engines likely causes lung cancer in humans and triggers a variety of other lung and respiratory illnesses. The study, the culmination of decades of research, highlights the health problems posed by the complex mix of gases and fine particles emitted by heavy-duty diesel engines operating on the nation's highways, farms and construction sites. "Overall, the evidence for a potential cancer hazard to humans resulting from chronic inhalation exposure to [diesel emissions] is persuasive," the report states.

Eric Pianin, "*EPA Links Lung Cancer, Diesel Exhaust*"
The Washington Post, September 4, 2002

Exposure to the pesticide methyl bromide and six other pesticides have been linked with an increased risk of prostate cancer among pesticide applicators in North Carolina and Iowa, U.S. government scientists reported Thursday. Methyl bromide is a fumigant gas used to protect crops from pests in the soil and to fumigate grain bins and other agricultural storage areas. Prostate cancer risks were two to four times higher among pesticide applicators than among men who were not exposed to methyl bromide.

Environment News Service,
"Methyl Bromide Exposure Raises Prostate Cancer Risk", May 1, 2003

Last year approximately 400,000,000 gallons of chemical termiticides were pumped onto American soil. That's enough chemical to fill 80,000 semi-tanker trucks.

"Current termite control practices are hazardous for new homeowners, who are not even required to be notified of toxic chemical use (soil poisons)," said Jay Feldman, executive director of the Washington, D.C.-based group Beyond Pesticides/National Coalition Against the Misuse of Pesticides.

A 2000 square foot home requires that 380 gallons of pesticide be pumped into the ground. In a 100-home subdivision, that's about 38 thousand gallons put where children and pets play, and the family gardens.

E-Wire Press, "Hidden Pesticide Hazards Lurk in Newly Built Homes"
April 17, 2002

Unborn U.S. babies are soaking in a stew of chemicals, including mercury, gasoline byproducts and pesticides, according to a report to be released Thursday. The report by the Environmental Working Group is based on tests of 10 samples of umbilical cord blood taken by the American Red Cross. They found an average of 287 contaminants in the blood, including mercury, fire retardants, pesticides and the Teflon chemical PFOA. "These 10 newborn babies were born polluted," said New York Rep. Louise Slaughter, who planned to publicize the findings at a news conference Thursday. "If ever we had proof that our nation's pollution laws aren't working, it's reading the list of industrial chemicals in the bodies of babies who have not yet lived outside the womb."

Maggie Fox, *"Unborn Babies Soaked in Chemicals, Survey Finds"*
Reuters, July 14, 2005

The nationwide price tag of perchlorate cleanup could be in the tens of millions, and possibly even billions, of dollars, according to water officials and other experts, who say it has the potential to dwarf California's problems with MTBE, a gasoline additive that tainted groundwater supplies. Perchlorate, which is highly soluble, has been detected in water supplies in California and at least 19 other states, usually near defense contractors or military bases. The Colorado River, which supplies drinking water to about 15 million people in the Southwestern United States, contains perchlorate that leached from the site of a former Nevada rocket fuel factory.

Miguel Bustillo, *"Lettuce Samples Found Tainted"*
Los Angeles Times, April 28, 2003

According to the latest data available from the American Wood Preservatives Institute's 1995 statistical report, about 1.6 billion pounds of wood preservatives are used to treat wood each year, including 138 million pounds of CCA, 656 million pounds of penta, and 825 million pounds of creosote. The three wood preservatives targeted by the lawsuit are linked to a wide range of health problems including cancer, birth defects, kidney and liver damage, disruption of the endocrine system and death. Two of the components of CCA, arsenic and chromium (VI), are classified as known human carcinogens. Creosote, a mix of toxic chemicals, is a cancer-causing agent and can cause nervous system damage.

Cat Lazaroff, *"U.S., Canada Groups Sue Over Toxic Wood Preservers"*
Environment News Service, December 11, 2002

Birds are being affected by lead on a massive scale. As of February 4, more than 176 trumpeter swans have been picked up dead or dying on the ponds they use in northern Washington State…it takes only three or four lead pellets to cause lead poisoning in a swan. Lead shotgun shells used for hunting contain about 280 lead pellets. For years, duck hunters left about 6,000 tons of lead shot annually in United States ponds, lakes and rivers before the US Fish and Wildlife Service banned its use in waterfowl hunting.

Jackie Alan Giuliano, Ph.D., *"Missing the Target-Green Bullets"*
Environment News Service, June 27, 2001

More than a quarter of the world's coral reefs have been destroyed by pollution and global warming, experts said Monday, warning that unless urgent measures are taken, most of the remaining reefs could be dead in 20 years. In some of the worst hit areas, such as the Maldives and Seychelles islands in the Indian Ocean, up to 90 percent of coral reefs have been killed over the past two years due to rises in water temperature. Coral reefs play a crucial role as an anchor for most marine ecosystems, and their loss would place thousands of species of fish and other marine life at risk of extinction.

Associated Press in the Deseret News,
"Coral reefs in grave peril, scientists say"
October 20, 2000

Frogs exposed to a mix of pesticides at extremely low concentrations like those widely found around farms suffer deadly infections, suggesting that the chemicals could be a major culprit in the global disappearance of amphibians, UC Berkeley scientists reported Tuesday. When tadpoles were exposed in laboratory experiments to each pesticide individually, 4 percent died before they turned into frogs. But when atrazine and eight other pesticides were mixed to replicate a Nebraska cornfield, 35 percent died. At least one-third of amphibians worldwide, or 1,856 of the known species of frogs, toads, salamanders and caecilians, are in danger of extinction, according to an international group of conservation biologists.

Marla Cone, *"A New Alarm Sounds for Amphibians"*
Los Angeles Times, January 25, 2006

Most oil pollution in North American coastal waters comes not from leaking tankers or oil rigs, but rather from countless oil-streaked streets. Additionally, sputtering lawn mowers and other dispersed sources on land, and so will be hard to prevent, said a panel convened by the National Academy of Sciences. The thousands of tiny releases, carried by streams and storm drains to the sea, are estimated to equal an Exxon Valdez spill — 10.9 million gallons of petroleum — every eight months. When fuel use on water, either inland or offshore, is also taken into account, the report says, about 85 percent of the 29 million gallons of marine oil pollution in North America each year comes from users — drivers, businesses, boaters — and not from the oil industry. In particular, spills from tankers, barges and other oil transport vessels totaled less than a quarter-million gallons in 1999, down from more than six million in 1990.

Andrew C. Revkin, *"Offshore oil pollution comes mostly as runoff"*
New York Times, May 24, 2002

The hole in the ozone layer over Antarctica is now three times larger than the United States — the biggest it's ever been, scientists at NASA said Friday. In a sign that ozone-depleting gases churned out years ago are just now taking their greatest toll, this year's South Pole ozone hole spreads over about 11 million square miles. Too much UV radiation can cause skin cancer and destroy tiny plants at the beginning of the food chain.

Associated Press reported on MSNBC.com,
"Largest ozone hole on record spotted", September 4, 2000

Thousands of idled farm workers [many from Mexico] are facing hunger in what has been a major center of California agriculture, hit by drought and court-ordered cutback of water supply to agriculture to protect endangered species (such as the Delta smelt). Water shortages cost California agriculture $260 million in 2007 as water deliveries fell to 35 percent of the routine level. The water shortage is expected to erase more than 55,000 jobs in the San Joaquin Valley. California has exceeded its sustainable water usage level for years, as its population rose from 10 million to 36 million in the last century.

Tracie Cone, *"Food Scarcity Even in US Produce Capital; Water Shortage Worst in three Decades"* Seattle Post-Intelligencer, December 13, 2008. p. A4.

Industrial vomit fills our skies and seas while pesticides and herbicides filter into our foods. Twisted automobile carcasses, aluminum cans, non-returnable glass bottles and synthetic plastics form immense middens in our midst as more and more of our detritus resists decay. We do not even begin to know what to do with our radioactive wastes—whether to pump them into the earth, shoot them into outer space, or pour them into the oceans. Our technological powers increase, but the side effects and potential hazards also escalate.

-Alvin Toffler, **Future Shock**, 1970

SECTION 6

ACTIONS AND SOLUTIONS

CHAPTER 38

//

INDIVIDUAL SOLUTIONS TO OUR DILEMMA

"If you want something done right, you have to do it yourself."

My Dad

An obvious question emerges: what fundamental component of our overpopulation crisis must be solved before our society and the rest of the world stands any chance of surviving this global "Human Katrina" population disaster?

Primary answer—in addition to sensible immigration control actions: *an alternative energy source to oil, coal and natural gas. An alternative energy source holds the key to survival for advanced civilizations on this planet. **It needs to be bio-alcohol that has been proven to be produced viably and in abundant quantities in 2021.** (www.biorootenergy.com)*

What's beyond methanol, ethanol, gasoline and diesel fuels?

Higher mixed alcohol fuel (a synthetic blend of linear, normal alcohols) contains about 60 percent more BTU's per unit volume than methanol, and nearly 20 percent more BTU's than ethanol. We use higher mixed alcohol fuel in today's gasoline and diesel engines as a blend stock or petroleum substitute in flex-fuel vehicles. (Source: Jay Toups, www.biorootenergy.com)

Why is it better?

Higher Mixed Alcohol Fuel

- Water, oil, and coal-soluble, biodegradable alcohol fuel formula
- 109-138 octane, depending on fuel blend
- Continuous 24×7 gas-to-liquid fuel synthesis, near zero process emissions
- Blends with gasoline, diesel and coal to increase combustion efficiency
- Suitable for use in all gasoline and diesel engines
- Use blended at 10-30 percent (gasoline engines) or up to 95percent in flex-fuel vehicles
- Use blended at 5-6 percent (diesel engines) for no black smoke and increased mileage
- Dramatically reduces tailpipe and smokestack emissions
- No engine modifications required for use in cars, trucks, ships, trains, planes, etc.
- Produced from all types of solid, liquid and gaseous carbon feedstocks
- Does not require planting, watering, harvesting and fermenting food crops

In order to create collective action to change current immigration inflow, the following organizations stand on the front line. Join them for free and take actions via their alerts with pre-written letters to your Congressional representatives. If you do nothing else, join www. NumbersUSA.com and add yourself to nearly 9.0 million members. You will be directed to send pre-written electronic faxes along with periodic phone calls to bring immigration back to sustainable numbers. Tell all your friends!

1. Join 9.0 million other Americans at www.numbersusa.com with director Roy Beck as one of the most effective and successful non-partisan organizations. Become a member of his fax/phone call armada of active citizens. Membership approaches nine million people, which harnesses a great deal of collective power. Distribute his five-minute video *"Immigration, Gumballs, and Poverty"* on

the web site to educate your networks as to the dangers of mass immigration.

2. Join www.fairus.org with Dan Stein at Federation of American Immigration Reform. He promotes sensible immigration reform that curtails mass immigration.

3. Join www.capsweb.org. Californians for Population Stabilization stands at the forefront in our most overpopulated state. They offer faxes and phone calls that empower citizens everywhere in the United States to take action on a proactive level. Very powerful and empowering to average citizens!

4. Join www.alipac.us with William Gheen to keep you on the front line of this national struggle. His member updates encourage local activism with the tools to make impact.

5. Join www.firecoalition.com with Jason Mrochek to bring information and tools to your fingertips. He stands on the front lines in California with members all over the country. Within that web site, you will find a half-dozen more effective web sites to take action.

6. Join www.grassfire.org with Steve Elliot for up-to-date information and actions you can take in your local areas.

7. Join www.cis.org or Center for Immigration Studies with Mark Krikorian for timely information on U.S. immigration impacts. Read Krikorian's ***The New Case Against Immigration: Both Legal and Illegal.***

8. Join www.limitstogrowth.org ; www.immigrationshumancosts.org with Brenda Walker to bring you outstanding information and data mostly squelched by mainstream media.

9. Join www.worldpopulationbalance.org with Dave Gardner and his team to keep you apprised of the global impacts of population.

10. Join www.populationmedia.org with Bill Ryerson for a firsthand look at what other countries experience as to overpopulation.

11. Join www.carryingcapacitynetwork.com and www.balance.org with David Durham for up to date and outstanding information and action items that you may use for very effective impact. Durham has worked for 35 years on this issue and continues to bring about sensible immigration to sustainable levels.

12. Join www.transitionus.ning.com ; www.transitiontowns.com to prepare yourself and your community for the post Peak Oil descent.

13. Join www.NPG.org for up to date information and well written essays on how to create negative population growth graciously and reasonably.

14. You will find excellent information in the following: www.plannedparenthood.org ; www.populationconnection.org ; www.care2.com ; www.world.org ; www.populationaction.org ; www.projectusa.org ; www.populationconnection.org ; www.proenglish.org

15. In Canada, www.actforcanada.org

16. In UK, www.populationmatters.com

17. In Australia, mark@australianpoet.com

Most of the aforementioned organizations offer speakers to invite to your local area.

One of the finest organizations offered: Dr. Jack Alpert of www.skil.org. We've been friends for 20 years. His brilliant videos educate anyone with compelling facts and realities we face as to human overpopulation. Copy and paste his videos to all your friends to educate them toward action.

The following information may be found at my website. You can forward it to your network of friends. They, in turn, can enlarge the network via their friends. This action letter covers individual and community actions available to all citizens.

ACTIONS YOU CAN TAKE TO CHANGE OUR COUNTRY TOWARD A SUSTAINABLE FUTURE!

Educate yourself on what we face and take action by joining these non-partisan organizations that empower you personally and collectively: www.numbersusa.com ; www.fairus.org www.capsweb.org ; www.firecoalition.com; www.alipac.us ; www.patriotunion.org ; www.cis.org

Contact top national shows by suggesting they interview experts on overpopulation such as Lester Brown, Richard Heinberg, Dr. Jack Alpert,

Fred Meyerson, Governor Richard D. Lamm, Kathleene Parker, Don Collins, Valerie Price, Madeline Weld, Anne Manetes, Dan Stein, Bob Dane, William Gheen, David Paxson, Dave Gardner, Buck Young, Frosty Wooldridge, Bill Ryerson, Jason Mrochek, and many others.

Write to: morning@npr.org ; 60m@cbsnews.com ; talk@npr.org Anderson Cooper at CNN, hannity@foxnews.com ; evening@cbsnews. com ; earlyshow@cbs.com ; special@foxnews.com ; today@nbc.com ; dateline@nbc.com ; letters@newsweek.com ; letters@time.com ; letters@ usnews.com ; editor@usatoday.com ; nightly@nbc.com ; late.edition@ cnn.com ; Norah O'Donnell at CBS, David Muir ABC, Lester Holt at NBC, Terry Gross at NPR, Steve Inskeep at NPR, Leslie Stahl at CBS, Bill Whittaker at CBS. Martha MacCallum, Dana Perino, Greg Gutfield and Jesse Waters at FOX NEWS. Wolf Blitzer at CNN. It's important to contact liberal, independent and conservative networks in order to educate everyone.

Environmentally, we must take action as to water, energy, air and land: www.wateruseitwisely.com ; www.treehugger.com ; www.willyoujoinus. com ; www.populationmedia.org ; www.ases.org for energy; www. greenpeace.org ; www.stopglobalwarming.org ; www.greenprintdenver. org ; www.mcs-global.org ; www.savetheoceans.org ; www.4oceans.org

What we must discuss: "U.S. Sustainable Population Policy"; "U.S. Carrying Capacity Policy"; "U.S. Environmental Impact Policy"; "U.S. Water Usage Policy." We must shift toward a sustainable, stable population for our civilization.

Personal actions: letters to the editor, speak at city council meetings to advance this information to fellow citizens, call local TV stations and ask to have state leaders on this issue interviewed in your state.

Arrange for a 45 minute meeting with your U.S. House Rep, U.S. Senator, State House Rep and State Senator. Inquire at my website for an outline covering that 45 minute presentation. Call into local radio stations in your community to take up the issue by interviewing experts on limits to water, clean air and highways.

Form clubs, groups and websites that make impact at the local level. Engage the media to report in your local papers.

Encourage other groups to host Frosty Wooldridge's *"THE COMING POPULATION CRISIS IN AMERICA: and how to change course*" or Roy Beck's "*IMMIGRATION BY THE NUMBERS*" or Dave Gardner "*World Population Balance.*" www.frostywooldridge.com; www.numbersusa.com ; www.worldpopulationbalance.org. Go to these websites for more action items.

Subscribe to **E-Magazine, Onearth, Greenpeace Magazine** and/or other environmental magazines that will inform you. Type into Google— "The top 100 environmental websites." You will receive information on the top 100 most effective websites on how you can take action.

These above actions will change consciousness in this country from unlimited growth and population gains to a stable, sustainable population. We must create the 'critical mass' of Americans that push this issue to the top of the presidential and congressional agendas. By gaining millions, we reach 'tipping point' that changes history.

Who is your hero? Susan B. Anthony? Dr. Martin Luther King? Gandhi? Eleanor Roosevelt? John Muir? Teddy Roosevelt? Amelia Earhart, Barbara Jordan? Joanne Wideman? Nellie Bly? They were common citizens with uncommon determination. That was their time, this is yours. You possess the same power to change history for the better. You are invited to bring your relentless enthusiasm and passion for your country, for your planet and in the end—for your children—to this noble task before all humanity.

Join thousands of citizens by becoming a national citizen press corps agent—with guidelines to engage media to interview leaders on overpopulation. For details, contact: frostyw@juno.com ; www.frostywooldridge.com

Books to inform:

Too Many People by Lindsey Grant
How Many Is Too Many by Phil Cafaro
A Bicentennial Malthusian *Essay* by John Rohe
The End of Nature by Bill McKibben
Out of Gas: The End of the Age of Oil by David Goodstein
The Long Emergency by James Howard Kunstler
The Population Bomb by Paul and Anne Ehrlich
Stalking the Wild Taboo by Garrett Hardin

The New Case Against Immigration: Both Legal and Illegal by Mark
    Krikorian
Our Plundered Planet by Fairfield Osborn
The Sixth Extinction by Leakey and Lewin
Food, Energy and Society by David and Marcia Pimentel
Biggest Lie Ever Believed by Michael Folkerth
Shoveling Fuel into a Runaway Train by Dr. Brian Czech
Peak Everything: Waking up to the Century of Declines by Richard
    Heinberg
***The Population Fix: Breaking America's Addiction to Population
Growth*** by Edward C. Hartman
The Transition Handbook: From Oil Dependency to Local Resilience
    by Rob Hopkins
***Blip: Humanity's 300-Year Self-Terminating Experiment with
Industrialism*** by Christopher O. Clugston
Scarcity: Humanity's Final Chapter by Christopher O. Clugston
Man Swarm and The Killing of Wildlife by Dave Foreman
America on the Brink: The Next Added 100 Million Americans by
    Frosty Wooldridge
Blackout: Coal, Climate and the Last Energy Crisis by Richard Heinberg
Together We Can Implement Change— watch "8 Billion Angels" shown
    in community screenings so that the topic of population is surrounded
    with meaningful dialogue that leads to personal introspection and
    powerful change. **www.8billionangeles.org** with **Terry Spahr**
Energy: www.biorootenergy.com with **Jay Toups**

What can you do to bring change?

You must become part of 'critical mass'—enough citizens writing,
calling, talking and promoting anyone who addresses this issue at the local,
state and national levels.

Our leaders have lost touch with you, and reality. They need your help.

We must spend billions for research on alternative energy to free us
from the grips of petroleum-oil. The thinking that got us into this mess
cannot be used to get us out. New paradigm brain-storming must begin.

Again, we need to move toward "bio alcohol" for our new alternative energy. www.biorootenergy.org

We cannot keep thinking that the solutions of the 20th century will solve our problems in the 21st century. They will not.

We must find solutions that work for the future of all humanity

We must stop fossil fuel burning as soon as possible. We must investigate both sides (in balance) of the climate change question, as soon as possible, then take decisive action and get to work on real solutions.

We must stop massive species extinction as soon as possible

We must balance our population— inside the carrying capacity of our nation and the planet— in order to bring about a sustainable society moving into the future.

Please, add your ideas to this basic list:

1. Possible alternatives show promise in solar conversion. Let's shift gears and engage ten times more top scientists to explore sunshine as our best non-polluting source of energy by changing it from light beams to electrical power. Let's engage wind power and wave power toward electrical power. Visit American Solar Energy Society in Boulder, Colorado at: www.ases.org.

2. Learn about the National Energy Research Laboratory (NREL) research and development of renewable fuels and electricity that advance national energy goals to change the way we power our homes, businesses, and cars.

    NREL's brand new "Wind to Hydrogen" facility offers new template for future energy production. Xcel Energy and NREL recently unveiled a unique facility that uses electricity from wind turbines to produce and store pure hydrogen, offering what may become an important new template for future energy production.

3. Produce only two and four-cylinder cars. Nobody needs a six or eight-cylinder car. I've been driving four-cylinder cars for a long time— starting with my VW in 1965. I've always arrived at my destination safely, and on time.

4. To promote more efficiency in the near future, we might promote possible incremental incentives:
    *   Charge $8.00 per gallon for all eight-cylinder cars
    * $6.00 a gallon for six-cylinder cars
    * $2.00 a gallon for four-cylinder cars
    * $1.00 a gallon for two-cylinder vehicles
    *   Push for more hybrid cars, with 70-100 miles per gallon.
    *   Push for electric cars, trucks, planes and more.

5. From that pricing-incentive approach, everyone would start moving toward greater efficiency, bicycling, carpools, bus, mass transit and ecological responsibility. If you think these ideas sound harsh, just wait until oil runs out— for greater trauma. If you've got better ideas, let's hear them! We must stop greenhouse gas emissions: www.stopglobalwarming.org. Please remember—more people make more greenhouse gases.

6. Create a nationwide bottle, can and plastic 50 cent deposit/return on every container sold at retail. That includes every container sold out of every store in America! No one loses a dime, and everyone becomes skilled recyclers! Money speaks louder than words.

7. Waste disposal: average Americans create around five pounds of waste daily. You may choose a number of waste-reducing methods.

    a. Bring your own cotton bags to grocery and retail outlets. I have cotton bags 37 years old and still hauling groceries!
    b. Vote to stop junk mail. www.stopjunk.com
    c. Use rechargeable batteries, or USB charged equipment.
    d. Buy "green" with less packaging.
        For more information, visit www.greenprintdenver.org for new ideas and how to start in your community. Use

that website for a template in your own state. Also, www.treehugger.com is an excellent site for environmental ideas and solutions.

8. How do you stop using chemicals that harm you and your family?
   a. Avoid any household product marked with "Caution"; "Warning"; "Danger."
   b. Use earth-friendly cleaners, purchased at your local stores.
   c. Dispose of hazardous waste by hauling to eco-recycle experts.
   d. Remember that everything you store in the house outgases into you and your children. Keep such chemicals in your garage.
   e. www.ecos.com ; www.melaleuca.com ; www.7thgeneration.com for safe cleaning products for your home. Also, www.mcs-global.org helps you deal with chemical poisoning.

9. We face a dreadful water crisis if we fail to stabilize our population. If we stopped all immigration today, our population momentum will add more than 35 million people within 29 years. Therefore, we must deal with our water issues.
   a. Practice water conservation with low flow flush toilets, water saver shower heads and know that every time you leave the tap running, it wastes water. www.wateruseitwisely.com
   b. Create xeriscape lawns-landscaping with minimum water needs. www.greenprintdenver.org and www.treehugger.com
   c. Move toward a healthier nutritional program by shifting toward more fruits, vegetables, grains and alternative protein products such as rice, beans, tofu and soy products to avoid more than 1,000 gallons of water and 16 pounds of grain used to produce one pound of beef.

10. Enjoy this revitalized thought-process; plug into like-minded people determined to make this planet livable. E-Magazine will give you up to the minute information. www.emagazine.com

11. Introduce environmental plans and ideas at your city council, church group and civic clubs.

12. Invest in solar power, wind power and other alternatives. Invest in solar heating panels on the roof of your house for heating water and rooms.

13. If we fail to find another energy source to power our infrastructure— to run our cars, power plants and home heating energy dependent civilizations around the planet will not survive.
    To promote healthy oceans, reefs and rainforests:
    www.savetheoceans.org and www.greenpeace.org

14. Visit this website for information leading to recycling programs in your area or find out how to start them in your community. www.recyclebank.com

Everything you do—counts!

Visit for 100 top web sites dealing with every method you can imagine for making your world a better place in which to live. www.world.org

To each passionate citizen reading this final part of the book, I invite you to act. If you take little or no action, your inaction creates impact— think about it!

Live in a state with lots of rivers? Protect them by adding your voice to www.americanrivers.org ; www.livinglandsandwaters.org

Finally, 900 cities around the world promote a new movement for all humanity. They move toward self-sustaining communities based on local production of food, shelter and goods. You may work toward a sustainable community in your area in America by contacting www.transitionus.ning.com. As our oil reserves decline, everyone will be forced to move toward smaller local communities that remain self-sustainable. The aforementioned website offers a complete protocol for nearly every state in the U.S.

Each day I sit in front of my keyboard, I read aloud the following to maintain momentum. I share it with you as we come together in this urgent action:

Until one is committed, there is hesitancy, the chance to draw back—always ineffectiveness. Concerning all acts of initiative and creation, there is one elementary truth—the ignorance of which kills countless ideas and splendid plans. That the moment one definitely commits oneself to a task, then Providence moves too—acting as one.

All sorts of things occur to help—that would never otherwise have occurred. A whole stream of events issues from the decision, raising in one's favor all manner of unforeseen incidents and meetings and material assistance, which no one could have dreamed would have come her/his way.

Whatever you can do, or dream you can do, begin it. Boldness has genius, power and magic in it. Begin it now!" Goethe (German philosopher)

All living creatures on earth thank you for your actions!

Addresses for your emails and letters asking those networks and individuals to interview top experts about America's overpopulation predicament:

Names and Addresses of National Media Networks:

60 Minutes
524 West 57th Street
NY, NY 10019
60M@cbsnews.com

Fox News
1211 Avenue of the Americas
NY, NY 10036

1 888 369 4762
Yourcomments@foxnews.com

Tucker Carlson
Jesse Waters
Greg Gutfield
Dana Perino
Sandra Smith
Martha MacCallum
Sean Hannity
Harris Faulkner
Arthel Neville

Foxfriends@foxnews.com
Ameriasnewsroom@foxnews.com
fncspecials@foxnews.com
foxaroundtheworld@foxnews.com
foxreport@foxnews.com
irena.briganti@foxnews.com
Cavuto@foxnews.com
Thestory@foxnews.com

CNN
190 Marietta St. NW
Atlanta, GA 30303

Or
CNN
1 CNN Center
Atlanta, GA 30303

Anderson Cooper
Erin Burnett
Wolf Blitzer
Brooke Baldwin
Zain Asher
Dana Bash
Anna Cabrera
Brianna Keilar
Melissa Knowles
Abby Phillip
Natasha Chen
Athena Jones
Christiane Amanpour
David Axelrod

PBS
2100 Crystal Dr.
Arlington, VA 22202

Colorado Public Radio
7409 Alton Court
Centennial, CO 80112

NPR
1111 North Capitol St. NE
Washington DC 20002

Terry Gross, Steve Inskeep, Robert Seigel

Npr.org/contact

Face the Nation
2020 M Street NW
W. DC 20036
ftn@cbsnews.com
202 457 4481

ABC News
47 West 66th Street
NY New York 10023

This Week
Good Morning America

Meet the Press
Lester Holt nightly@nbcuni.com

Contact.mtp@nbcuni.com
Todaystories@nbcuni.com
Dateline.contactus@nbcuni.com
msnbctvinfo@nbcuni.com
Jason.abbruzzesc@nbcuni.com

If you would like to book this program in your city, please contact as shown below:

Title of the presentation: "THE COMING POPULATION CRISIS IN AMERICA: and HOW TO CHANGE COURSE"

The USA will double its population from 330 million to over 439 million sometime past mid-century and 625 million by 2095—if current growth rates continue. It will add 100 million within 29 years by 2050. Demographic predictions show Colorado adds five million people to the Front Range in the next 40 years. California will add 20 million within the next 30 years. Texas will add 12 million. We create an irreversible crisis with unsolvable problems for our children.

"The problems in the world today are so
enormous they cannot be solved with the level
of thinking that created them." Einstein

Frosty Wooldridge, former Colorado math/science
teacher, and author of 15 books, has bicycled 100,000

miles on six continents and 15 times across the United States coast to coast in the past 45 years. He has witnessed the crisis of overpopulation in Mexico, China, Bangladesh, India and South America.

He presents a clear picture of the future for America if we continue on this Titanic-like course, while offering solutions that stand in line with Einstein's appreciation for stepping out of the box. He presents a powerful and compelling program to all audiences laced with humor, compassion and sense of optimism. Wooldridge has been a guest on hundreds of radio and TV programs across the United States including ABC, CBS, NBC and FOX.

As Eleanor Roosevelt said, "We must prevent human tragedy

rather than run around trying to save ourselves after an event has already occurred. Unfortunately, history clearly shows that we arrive at catastrophe by failing to meet the situation, by failing to act when we should have acted. The opportunity passes us by, and the next disaster is always more difficult and compounded than the last one."

You may choose the one-hour program or the 1.25-hour program that includes dramatic world travel slide show that takes audiences from the Arctic to Antarctica.

Wooldridge distributes information whereby every person in the audience may take action on a personal level to ensure a viable future for our children and the United States.

Frosty Wooldridge
frostyw@juno.com
www.frostywooldridge.com
www.HowToLiveALifeOfAdventure.com

CHAPTER 39

//

ACTIONS AT THE NATIONAL LEVEL

"In the current instance, the rational basis for the appeal, and its centrality to our survival, are clear. Nothing is to be lost and everything to be gained by sharing accurate and relevant information about our situation; there is no need to exaggerate the threat."

Richard Heinberg, Peak Everything

Where do we start? What on earth can anyone do to change the grave results of adding 100 million people to the United States by 2050? What about the fact that the rest of humanity expects another 3.0 billion added by 2050? Why won't our leaders speak up about an issue so dire that it affects every American today and in the future?

Why wouldn't we question U.S. population growth when millions sit in gridlock traffic, breathe toxic air, pay more for everything, suffer water shortages—and know that it can only worsen?

Heck of a Question! Everyone Runs from the Answer

As you can imagine—religions, emotions, cultures and history lock most humans into paradigms formed 2,000 years ago. While such paradigms fail in the 21st century, most humans cling to those beliefs as a life raft in the desert when they must search for water. Capitalism, corporations and religions postulate that humans can multiply forever. That premise shall prove our greatest obstacle to reasonable choices.

As you read this information, you realize our civilization stands at grave risk. What can you do?

In all of recorded history, passionate men and women rose out of nowhere to take action to right some wrong. Some became famous while most did not. Fame meant nothing to them other than it became a byproduct of their actions. Another aspect of their work rendered what Malcolm Gladwell called a "tipping point" in history where change occurred via the bravery and passion of common persons with uncommon determination.

That "tipping point" became critical mass that provoked American colonists to fight and die for their new country. Susan B. Anthony provided a "tipping point" to gain voting rights for women. In India, Gandhi's walk to the sea provided a "tipping point" to oust the British. Dr. Martin Luther King provoked the civil rights movement.

Which great person in history inspires you? John Muir? Betsy Ross, Teddy Roosevelt? Nellie Bly? Charles Lindbergh? Amelia Earhart? Harry Truman? Jane Goodall? Your dad? Your mom? What do they all possess in common? Noble purpose!

That Was Their Time; This Is Yours

You're invited to bring your highest creative energy to this noblest hour in history. What we do in the next decade will change the course of history for America and the world. That can mean for better or worse, depending on our collective actions.

How can we stop the United States from adding 100 million people?

In this chapter of the book, we'll examine logical, practical and reasonable choices to stabilize America's population to a sustainable future for all citizens. By taking actions for ourselves, we will inspire and invite other countries to establish their own choices.

Since the U.S. female has enjoyed a 2.03 fertility level since 1970, it's not America growing its population from within. What causes our accelerating population growth? Short answer: both legal and illegal immigration, in addition to their birth rates.

Since you own or rent your dwelling, you may choose to invite 20 guests or 100 guests depending on your available space. We as a nation must choose how many guests we can sustain in our "house."

Since legal and illegal immigration constitute the main sources of our population crisis, we must act to diminish the cause of over 2.4 million immigrants added annually.

Yes, our actions will force overloaded nations to reconsider, change and solve their own population challenges. Is it unreasonable for national and personal responsibility?

What we must enact:

1. A TWENTY YEAR MORATORIUM ON ALL IMMIGRATION: This would allow our country to regain its collective breath. It would allow us to regain our schools, language, medical facilities, financial balance, ecological viability and order, which is necessary for a first world country to operate for all its citizens.

   We must employ a linkage strategy. In other words, we must create a paradigm shift that employs all the following actions to reap a plausible future for our citizens in America. A former congressman said, "The challenge is enormous, and you have to talk about a moratorium. You can't talk about anything short of a moratorium because, frankly, anything less will never get you one step closer to population stabilization."

   After the 20 year immigration moratorium, we install an "Egress Equals Ingress" policy; if 50,000 people vacate America in a year, we can allow 50,000 to migrate onto our shores—with needed skills to our benefit—that speak the English language before they arrive—they will be considered for the United States. If that maintains our stable population, we can continue.

   We could entertain a farm guest worker program only if it stipulates that male workers enjoy an entry date for three months to a maximum of six months, plus an exit date. No female or family members allowed. Additionally, no 'instant birthright citizenship' allowed for foreign nationals' babies born on U.S. soil.

   Yes, we must work with Americans marrying foreign spouses

and a few other visa considerations, but we must hold to our limited carrying capacity.

As far as foreign visitors, we need a visa tracking system to ensure that such guests enter our country and exit on a specific date or face criminal charges, and jail.

2.   NATIONAL SUSTAINABLE POPULATION POLICY for the United States of America: How many people can this nation hold and still maintain our standard of living and quality of life? How can we maintain it in order to provide the "American Dream" opportunity for all U.S. citizens? How can we maintain enough water and farmland to feed ourselves instead of depending on elusive imports from other countries as global climate change and gasoline become more critical? What is our population limit?

3.   NATIONAL ENVIRONMENTAL IMPACT POLICY for the United States of America: The U.S. and all countries must deal with the harsh reality of limited human population. As head of the free world, we must lead in the understanding that a national population policy will give future generations a sustainable planet. Without it, we drive forward with no idea of where we're heading and where we'll end up. China is already where we don't want to go, and India is even worse because it keeps driving its civilization over a cliff as it adds another 300 million by 2050. We must move toward two children or less family policy. We can do it by choice today because we're already at 2.03 children per American female. If we wait, we'll be in the same boat as the Chinese with forced one child per family.

Of course, religious leaders will scream 'abortion' and other critical name calling. No! A population policy gifts us with choices for birth control before our civilization runs out of options. Or, do we and church leaders prefer millions dying of starvation annually as they wallow in misery from hyper-population growth?

When anyone talks about stabilizing America's population, the first terms you hear: racist, xenophobe and nativist. Please understand this fact: Mother Nature doesn't care about your race, creed or color when she runs out of food, energy and resources to sustain you. Once you understand that FACT, no more name-calling works.

In addition, we must enact a state-by-state policy—I live in Colorado, so a "Colorado Sustainable Population Policy" to determine how many people can live in Colorado within the water, food, land and resources in my state. "Colorado Environmental Impact Policy" to determine how many people will allow enough land and habitat for animals in Colorado. Every state must develop these policies along with a "Water Usage Policy."

Additionally, we must move toward a national 50 cent deposit recycling law on every piece of plastic, glass and metal sold out of retail stores to guarantee 99.9 percent recycling to stop the carnage of our environment with throwaways.

4. FAMILY PLANNING WORLDWIDE: The United States and other first world countries need to assist other countries with family planning methods. Birth control is a major aspect of family planning. Without it, third world countries suffer endless population increases and degradation. During one of my lectures a student asked, "How can we force other countries to have two child families…isn't that overstepping our bounds?"

To answer that question, I said, "Correct! We can never infringe on other cultures or countries. We can only offer them the means and ability to bring their societies into population homeostasis. Should they choose otherwise, they will find that Nature proves to be the ultimate population arbiter."

Lester Brown, *Plan B 4.0*, wrote: "Population growth, which contributes to all the problems discussed here, has its own tipping point. Scores of countries have developed enough economically to sharply reduce mortality but not yet enough to reduce fertility. As a result, they are caught in the demographic trap—a situation where rapid population growth begets poverty and poverty begets rapid population growth. In this situation, countries eventually tip one way or the other. They either break out of the cycle or they break down."

To subsist, the Catholic Church, Protestants, Buddhists, Hindu, Islam and other religions that continually work against family planning—must step out of the Dark Ages and into the 21st century. We can promote education that spotlights and unhinges their entrenched thinking based on concepts that formed 2,000 years ago. Humans can no longer usurp Nature's laws via hyper-population growth.

It's not logical to think any of these great religions would flip toward rational action by accepting family planning any time soon. Therefore, we must take care of our citizens first to ensure our country's viability. After that, we may continue our assistance worldwide.

5. DEVELOPMENTAL ASSISTANCE: First world countries need to assist with development, housing, education, fresh water, family planning and health care for countries that suffer from this planet-wide population crisis. Help them in their own countries. That means tractors, crop techniques, irrigation, etc. No financial aid because money tends to go into the hands of the leaders.

6. ELECT SENATORS AND CONGRESSIONAL REPRESENTATIVES WHO REPRESENT AMERICANS: One of the reasons Congress and our presidents have created this national atrocity stems from their entrenchment in the 'good old boy' network in Washington DC. As long as they represent massive immigration as well as corporations who pander to this predicament, you will not see change. You must elect leaders who will take action on behalf of Americans, and really, humanity. The best solution: Term Limits to move newer, fresher and more worldly people into the halls of power.

A scant 50 percent of Americans vote in national elections. Local elections rate less than 20 percent participation most of the time. More Americans see this crisis and step up to the plate. They must run for office in many states.

7. The most important factor for saving America, and really, the planet: **you!** Use the Internet with websites that create collective action. Connect with all Americans! Use your money and your time! Stand up! Write! Call! Educate on radio talk shows! Call on TV networks and express your concerns. Express your ideas! Be heard! Be seen! Be passionate! Demand! Expect action! Become action in motion! Instead of watching the news, become the news by your actions!

CHAPTER 40

///

INTERNATIONAL ACTIONS

"To waste, to destroy our natural resources, to skin and exhaust the land instead of using it so as to increase its usefulness, will result in undermining in the days of our children the very prosperity which we ought by right to hand down to them amplified and developed."
Theodore Roosevelt

This blue-green orb whirling through the universe proves an amazing creative wonder to any human being that looks up into the night sky. As the morning sunlight bursts across the eastern horizon, seldom do other species take special notice. But for humans, the drama unfolds in light banners, streamers, blazing clouds and an array of creative processes.

Perhaps our planet-home may be a fluke of the universe but, as much as we know, this sphere proves to be the only game in town. There is no Planet B.

Additionally, we find, as humans, our destructive actions threaten not only fellow life forms on this globe, but our long-term existence.

In the past 100 years, we wreaked havoc on this planet with chemicals, fossil fuel burning and overpopulation of our species. We conquered nature by destroying its balancing systems. As a consequence, today, our "Human Katrina" created a "Human Dilemma" from which we must engage "Human Solutions."

Otherwise, the nature of Mother Nature dictates harsher and harsher results.

What responsibility do we possess for future generations?

In a simple statement: we owe our progeny, as well as all living creatures on this spaceship-home—a livable, viable and sustainable planet that we inherited.

How can we do that as a collective effort worldwide?

1. Leaders from all countries or as many major nations as can be incorporated—must form an international conference and coalition of governments coming together with a theme of "*World Population Stability for a Sustainable Future for All Living Creatures on Planet Earth.*"

2. We must include religious leaders, climate change specialists, population experts, resource specialists, water experts, species extinction experts, habitat experts, glacier experts, river specialists, insect experts and any other experts to bring their knowledge to the table. They must create and evolve a viable plan for stabilizing world population via education, birth control and family planning. They must hammer out a consensus for future generations. They must gather the world's brightest minds to create an alternative energy source to supplant oil as soon as possible. They must address species extinction and climate change. They must move humanity toward quality of life and environmental balance while working with human and animal dignity.

3. The richest and/or most populated nations may host the conference(s) in order to create a world plan. If no nation will step forward to host such a conference, the United States must take the lead by inviting as many nations to this world summit as will accept.

4. While they may introduce several viable paradigms, Lester Brown, president of Earth Policy Institute, wrote, **PLAN B 4.0**, which offers one of the finest, most refined approaches for saving civilizations around the planet.

5. **Once a 'critical mass' of nations sign on with, *PLAN B 4.0*, or some form thereof, humanity can move toward a sustainable future based on population stability and 'steady state economics'.**

Think back 29 years! What did you do with your life? What meaningful triumphs? What childhood bliss did you enjoy? How about the high points of your high school and college years, or first job? Later, picture your kids graduating from high school or college. How about that trip to your favorite destination? How quickly did 29 years slip into your scrapbooks?

How old will you be 29 years from now? Forty-five? Fifty-five? Sixty-five? How much space, resources and energy that paint your 'ideal' future will have been constricted by hyper-population growth—if you and your government fail to act?

Whether we like it or not, our civilization depends on choices manifested by every single citizen's individual actions today. Hopefully, this book enlightened you and catapulted you to take action at whatever level you feel empowered—so your dreams or your children's dreams 29 years from now may enjoy scrapbook memories.

The End

INDEX

(1) www.theoceancleanup.com ; Over 5 trillion pieces of plastic currently litter the ocean. Trash accumulates in five ocean garbage patches, the largest one being the Great Pacific Garbage Patch, located between Hawaii and California. If left to circulate, the plastic will impact our ecosystems, health, and economies.

(2) www.ourworldindata.org ; Of the 56.9 million deaths worldwide in 2016, more than half (54%) were due to the top 10 causes. Ischemic heart disease and stroke are the world's biggest killers, accounting for a combined 15.2 million deaths in 2016. These diseases have remained the leading causes of death globally in the last 15 years.

(3) www.condorferries.co.uk ; There is now 5.25 trillion macro and micro pieces of plastic in our global oceans and 46,000 pieces float on every square mile of ocean, weighing up to 269,000 tons. Every day around 8 million pieces of plastic makes their way into our oceans.

(4) www.cis.org or Center for Immigration Studies, Dr. Steven Camarota; www.NumbersUSA.org, Roy Beck

(5) www.skil.org ; Dr. Jack Alpert

(6) wwf.panda.org ; Experts calculate that between 0.01 and 0.1 percent of all species will become extinct each year. If the low estimate of the number of species out there is true-i.e., That means approximately 8,760 extinctions occur every year. Note: driven by human encroachment, habitat destruction and chemical contamination.

(7) Source: Life Magazine, August 1991, Shark Alert! The age-old struggle between man and shark has become a killing frenzy. We are slaughtering 100 million every year, driving them to extinction.

(8) www.pewsocialtrends.org ; Though overall U.S. birth rates ticked up just prior to the recession, in the long term, they have declined noticeably. In 1970 the rate was 88.5 births per 1,000 women of childbearing age, and after hitting a historical low of 62.3 in 2013, rates inched up for the first time since the recession in 2014, to 62.8. Current US birth rate per woman in 2020: 1.8 children.

(9) www.NumbersUSA.org ; Roy Beck, Immigration off the Charts, http://www.youtube.com/watch?v=muw22wTePqQ

(10) Population growth is the increase in the number of individuals in a population. Global human population growth, net gain, amounts to around **83 million** annually, or 1.1 percent per year. The global population has grown from 1 billion in 1800 to 7.8 billion in 2020. www.ourworldindata.org

(11) www.ourworldindata.org ; China contributes the highest share of mismanaged plastic waste with around 28 percent of the global total, followed by 10 percent in Indonesia, 6 percent for both the Philippines and Vietnam. Other leading countries include Thailand (3.2 percent); Egypt (3 percent); Nigeria (2.7 percent) and South Africa (2 percent). Estimates of plastic pieces in the oceans range from 5.25 trillion pieces of plastic to as many as 6.1 trillion with 8 million more pieces added 24/7.

(12) www.ncbi.nim.nih.gov ; **In India, diarrhea kills 2,195 children every day—more than AIDS, malaria, and measles combined. Diarrheal diseases account for 1 in 9 child deaths worldwide, making diarrhea the second leading cause of death among children under the age of 5.**

(13) www.npr.org ; Every year, around 9 million people die of hunger, according to the international relief agency Mercy Corps. That's more than the death toll of AIDS, malaria and tuberculosis combined. May 5, 2020

(14) www.theborgenproject.org ; The Borgen Project tackles key global data about starvation and malnutrition. Approximately 3.1 million children die of hunger each year.

(15) www.worldhealthorganization.org ; Billions of people around the world are continuing to suffer from poor access to water, sanitation and hygiene, according to a new report by UNICEF and the World

Health Organization. Some 2.2 billion people around the world do not have safely managed drinking water services, 4.2 billion people do not have safely managed sanitation services, and 3 billion lack basic handwashing facilities.

(16) www.MacroTrends.net ; In 2019, annual population growth in China amounted to about 0.33 percent on 1.4 billion. That equates to 8,000,000 net gain annually.

(17) www.cs.mun.ca ; The area around the Yangtze River and Pearl River estuaries was listed as marine dead zones in 2006 in a United Nations Study. Fertilizers introduced into the water from farms further upstream caused the growth of the algae to be accelerated and augmented the problem. In the United Nations report it was stated that 500,000 tons of ammonia nitrogen and 30,000 tons of phosphate entered the ocean through the Yangtze River in 2005. In June of 2005 the red algae blooms had affected about 1000 km^2 of the ocean around the Yangtze River mouth.

(18) www.populationof.net/bangladesh ; Total Bangladesh population should reach 169,775,000 by 2020 and should increase to **201,927,000** people by year 2050. The life expectancy at birth should reach 80.4 (78.8 years for male and 82.0 years for females). Population density will go up to 1,551.3 people per square kilometer.

(19) www.cbpp.org ; The Supplemental Nutrition Assistance Program (SNAP, formerly known as food stamps) is the nation's most important anti-hunger program, reaching 38 million people nationwide in 2019 alone.

(20) www.who.int ; Contaminated water transmits diseases such diarrhea, cholera, dysentery, typhoid, and polio. Contaminated drinking water is estimated to cause 485,000 diarrheal deaths each year. By 2025, half of the world's population will be living in water-stressed areas.

(21) www.usgs.gov ; On average, each person uses about 80-100 gallons of water per day, for indoor home uses. Are you surprised that the largest use of household water is to flush the toilet, and after that, to take showers and baths?

(22) www.cowspiracy.com ; Facts and figures concerning the beef industry.

(23) www.statista.com ; Some 273.6 million vehicles were registered in US in 2018. The figures include passenger cars, motorcycles, trucks,

buses, and other vehicles. The number of cars sold in the U.S. per year stood at **6.3 million** in 2016.

(24) www.350.org ; January 26, 2017, Nicoloa Jones, Last year will go down in history as the year when the planet's atmosphere broke a startling record: 400 parts per million of carbon dioxide. The last time the planet's air was so rich in $CO2$ was millions of years ago, back before early predecessors to humans were likely wielding stone tools; the world was a few degrees hotter back then, and melted ice put sea levels tens of meters higher.

(25) www.hcn.org ; Feb 7, 2005 — 1 million. Number of vertebrates run over each day in the United States (a rate of one death every 11.5 seconds).

(26) www.ourworldindata.org ; According to calculations using baseline data from 2011, global demand for seafood destined for human consumption is 143.8 million tons per year, and the overall consumption footprint, which also includes other uses of seafood, is 154 million tons.

(27) Sources: National Interagency Fire Center; CalFire; Maricopa County; National Weather Service; National Centers for Environmental Information; National Water Information System (USGS); Energy Information Administration; Oregon Department of Forestry; Environmental Protection Agency; Western Regional Climate Center; United States Drought Monitor.

(28) www.wikapedia.org ; Definitions of quality of life.

ABOUT THE AUTHOR

Frosty Wooldridge lives each day with gratitude, boundless enthusiasm and a sense of purpose for everything he undertakes. He graduated from Michigan State University in journalism/advertising. He earned a post graduate degree in English Literature from Grand Valley State University, Allendale, Michigan. He loves mountain climbing, scuba diving, swing dancing, skiing and bicycle touring. He has rafted, canoed, backpacked, sailed, windsurfed, snowboarded and more all over the planet. He has bicycled 100,000 miles on six continents and 15 times across the United States. His feature articles have appeared in national and international magazines for 40 years. He writes and speaks on overpopulation and environmental challenges facing humanity. He has taught at the elementary, high school and college levels. He has interviewed on NBC, CBS, ABC, CNN, FOX and 1,500 radio shows in the past 20 years. His website contains more information for anyone aspiring toward a spectacular life:

www.HowToLiveALifeOfAdventure.com

Facebook adventure pages:

Frosty Wooldridge
How to Live a Life of Adventure: The Art of Exploring the World
Bicycle Touring Unique Moments
Bicycling Poets
America's Overpopulation Predicament

Acknowledgements: Sandi Lynn for editing, ideas and support during the arduous research for this book. Thank you Jim Ament and Tim

Davis for valued comments. Thank you Bromwell Ault for your wisdom. Thank you to Fred Elbel for my websites, editing and ideas. Thank you to Cynthia Schoen for ideas and concepts. Thank you Rex Wooldridge for wise feedback on current events. Thank you Jack Alpert for your continuous education on this topic. Thank you Chris Clugston for your brilliant analysis of humanity's predicament. Thank you Bob Dane for years of excellent feedback. Thank you Dell Erickson for your research on energy. Thank you Ken Hampshire for your steadfast understanding and brilliant writing. Thank you Dave Paxson for your lifetime of educating Americans concerning world overpopulation and solutions. Thank you Joanne Wideman for your leadership at CAPS. Additionally, thank you Debbie Rohe, Jenny Goldie and Linda Purdue for all your work and efforts over the decades. Thank you John Stchur for wise counsel and a life-long friendship. Thank you Don Collins and Sally Epstein for your steadfast determination to bring safe, effective birth control to the world's poor.

Book cover: Gridlocked traffic on I-25 north and southbound on 20th Street in Denver, Colorado. Six days a week, vehicle traffic on I-70, I-225, C-470, and I-25 grinds along bumper-to-bumper at three to five mph. While drivers fume in gridlocked traffic, they breathe toxic air from the famous Brown Cloud 24/7. Police reports show an average of 20 to 30 accidents 24/7 in all Denver traffic. On weekends, I-70 into the mountains to the camping sites and ski resorts takes three hours to drive 90 miles to Vail, Copper, Breckenridge, Keystone, A-Basin and Loveland. Coming home on Sunday turns into a 6 hour ordeal of bumper-to-bumper. Yet, Denver expects to jump from 2.7 million to 4.7 million within 29 years. That photograph represents all metropolitan cities in America where the gridlocked traffic has become tiresome, dangerous and guaranteed to worsen beyond solving. Photography by Frosty Wooldridge

Praise for: **America's Overpopulation Predicament: Blindsiding Future Generations** by Frosty Wooldridge

"With an unmatched passion propelled by pedal power – the thousands of miles he has pedaled his bicycle through scores of countries around the planet – the incomparable, almost larger-than-life Frosty Wooldridge draws on his firsthand experiences to issue a jeremiad about the perils of overpopulation. In developing countries such as India and Niger, overpopulation tends to be caused by "natural" increase (an excess of births over deaths), while in developed countries like the United States and Canada, it is caused by high rates of immigration. In both cases, it is unsustainable. At a time when humanity as a whole is living beyond our ecological means – in what ecologists call a state of "overshoot" – every year, we continue to add more than 80 additional people to an already overstressed biosphere. Each newcomer, like each person already here, is a consumer of overexploited natural resources and an emitter of wastes, including climate-altering carbon dioxide and poisonous toxics. Ever the diehard optimist though, Frosty spells out what YOU can do to help make a difference between survival and collapse for both civilization and the biosphere."

Leon Kolankiewicz, environmental scientist

While reading Frosty Wooldridge's **America's Overpopulation Predicament: Blindsiding Future Generations**, it becomes increasingly clear that Wooldridge knows his subject so uniquely and so well that there would be little point, if any, in arguing with him. It also will probably grow upon the reader that had our planet's political leaders had the same interests and sense of discovery driving them as Frosty possesses, our human race would have a far better understanding of the present and view of the future.

"Wooldridge's life has been extraordinary by any standard. He has been a farmer, teacher, truck driver, author, lecturer and world traveler at the ground level, having bicycled across six of our seven continental land masses. All else ––––jungles, deserts, mountains, cities, –––––– offered him the chance to see the human race and its problems wherever he rode from a height of about six feet. Whatever problems he encountered, whether caused by wealth, poverty religion, warfare, drought, starvation, disease etc., he could always view them and their consequences from close-up.

"Not surprisingly, Wooldridge places human overpopulation in its rightful place at the center of our global predicament ————— one that finds most cultures except some "primitive" ones recklessly pursuing uncontrolled growth in an environment of fixed natural resources. And Wooldridge, at his unique elevation of sea level plus six, guides us to the conclusion that our overpopulation is more than a predicament. It is a disaster in the making. **America's Overpopulation Predicament** ... is a "must read" in anyone's survival kit." Bromwell Ault, author

"A powerful and stark 'Big-picture' warning. Wooldridge's rhetorical grasp draws together for all to understand, the unsustainable trajectory humanity is set on and warns that if we don't 'wake up' urgently to the challenges we must tackle, life on our planet as we know it will descend into a ravaged dystopia." Brian McGavin, environmentalist

"Wow! The breadth, scope, organization and inarguable logic contained in this book is so impressive that you simply must read it for the same reason that an opportunity to experience the best of the best in any field is something not to be missed. But there are lots of other reasons as well. Dead serious reasons. He lays it all out for the reader so convincingly and in such an impossible-to-ignore, impossible to rationalize away fashion that I, for one, am determined to do my part to implement solutions. Luckily, Wooldridge offers some extremely well thought-out, "doable" strategies to do just that! Oh, and did I mention impeccable documentation backing every fact, every statement and the passion evident throughout his writing? In short, this is a book that everyone who cares about the future should read, and politicians and policy-makers should read it multiple times!" John Stchur, teacher

"**The Population Bomb** by Paul Ehrlich published in 1968 when the world population tabulated at 3.5 billion humans. America and the world ignored it. Ehrlich and his wife wrote **The Population Explosion** in 1990. America and the world ignored it. More and more books cropped up like Richard Heinberg's **Peak Everything,** which was ignored, too. In 2012, Christopher Clugston wrote **Scarcity: Humanity's Final Chapter.** Again, everyone ignored it. There are a dozen books on what America faces as to water shortages, the end of oil and resource depletion. This book by Mr. Wooldridge spells out the future SO graphically, you can't ignore it. As he says in his Introduction, your kids' futures await your actions today to mitigate what's coming. If America ignores this book, it's getting to be too late in the game to save our civilization. These are dire times. We need effective solutions. This book offers a chance for the future." Barbara Cook, salon operator

"If you are a parent, you need to read this book. If you're a U.S. Senator or Congressperson, this book will change the way you look at population growth, all forms of immigration and what your kids face in the future. If you're the governor of a state, you need to read this book. If you care about America's environment, this book spells out how to preserve it. This book is not for the faint of heart. It hits hard on what our country faces. If you project your own kids' future 30 years from now, it's quite frightening to imagine them living in our country with an added 100 million more people. It's not comforting what Wooldridge describes is coming. Thankfully, he offers solutions. We all need to take action." Janice Scott, housewife

"I couldn't put this book down. The author grabbed me by the throat in the Introduction. He didn't let loose of me until the last page. By looking around you, there's no way to stand in denial of what America faces in three short decades. Our country needs to make some very big changes, immediately! This book is a towering lighthouse warning us about the future and how to steer clear of the rocks. I hope enough people heed this book's warnings." Arnold Bostwick, college student

"This book knocked me backward mentally and emotionally. It's like I opened up a tube of toothpaste with no way to stop the flow of knowledge. Each chapter blew my mind. We face serious problems that no longer can be ignored. What's 30 years? Since I am retired, I can tell you, 30 years go by in a blink. With Wooldridge's documentation, we can't outrun nor can we flee this population-monster bearing down on America. I would recommend this book to every mother and father in the country. Please take action for your children." Paula Harris, retired teacher

"If you have younger children or grandchildren who face the consequences of the overpopulation time bomb described by Wooldridge, you must read his most recent book on the topic and consider what you can do at the local, state and national levels to encourage your legislators to become more knowledgeable about how they can influence passage of rational immigration policies. The book offers numerous strategies and tactics for you to use as you join others to stop the avalanche before the country is overwhelmed. These are the people who quickly becoming dependent on the government and cost billions for food, housing and medical support, and their numbers grow exponentially. Rather than allow this lawless hoard to continue to grow, pressure needs to be applied to legislators to pass policies which will slow down illegal entry. Three cheers for calling attention to one of the most serious and most overlooked problems facing America today." Dr. Gary North, retired college administrator

"I have been privileged to read about Wooldridge's amazing travels and experiences around the world. Therefore, unlike many people without such broad exposure to our planetary situation, we take from this latest book strong reasons for concern for the future. When I was born in 1931 the US population was about 130 million, and it is now close to 340 million while world numbers in the same span of time have gone from 2 billion to almost 8 billion. We have many colleagues who have written about the impossibility of adding many more to a finite planet as we continue to ravage its non-renewable resources.

"Voices such as E. O Wilson and Sir David Attenborough remind us of the global warming disasters ahead.

"I am somewhat heartened by the stated objectives of the Biden Administration, but actions always speak louder than words. Thus, Wooldridge's continuing efforts with this powerful new book must be welcomed and promoted as I attempted to do with my endorsement here.

New ideas for how to win the stability we seek must emerge. For example, the arrival of battery powered vehicles offers some respite from the fossil fuel pollution now raising global temperatures to highly dangerous levels.

Global leadership must be harnessed to accomplish significant goals which must include the improvement of lives of so many now living on the edges of starvation and disease." Don Collins, writer, world traveler

Wooldridge vividly describes the assault of our species on the planet that sustains us as we career along our trajectory of overshoot. Human population continues to grow rapidly while our giant economy devours irreplaceable non-renewable resources, and renewable resources, faster than they can be replenished. We encroach on wildlife habitat, disrupt ecosystems, and injure the planet with multiple forms of pollution. Despite all this, billions remain poor and hungry. Wooldridge makes clear that overpopulation in poor countries cannot be solved through migration to rich countries. Additionally, rich countries must curb their consumption. A finite planet can support neither an ever-growing population nor an ever-expanding economy. Relentless growth is not making our lives better, but more stressful. The future may not be pretty whatever we do, but if we do nothing to slow and reverse human population growth, it will be far worse. Madeline Weld, President, Population Institute Canada

"Every person concerned about their children, grandchildren and great-grandchildren must, and I do mean MUST, read this book. This book sets forth, in simple terms, every fact and concept every human being must understand in order to prevent the collapse of civilization with the deaths of billions that will occur in the very near future, if action is not taken today. The author's research is seen on every page of the book and clearly shows the effort the author put into the book for the benefit of the reader.

"Humans must tackle the most difficult problem that humanity has ever faced since evolving from the apes. And the author of the book goes to great lengths to make you, the reader, understand the problem. That problem is very simple—with the fact that the earth is finite and can only provide humanity with limited resources. Combined with the exploding human population, action must be taken today to prevent the collapse of civilization with the deaths of billions." Jason Brent, Judge, CPA, Attorney, author of: **Humans: An Endangered Species**

"Population growth worsens our most serious problems—climate change, economic inequality, resource depletion, pollution, and loss of wild nature. And the impacts of growth are worst in countries where per-capita consumption is highest, like the US. It's time we had a national conversation, and this is the book to ignite it." Richard Heinberg

Senior Fellow, Post Carbon Institute, author of: **Peak Everything, Blackout, Our Renewable Future**

Other books by the author:

Handbook for Touring Bicyclists—Bicycling touring grows in popularity each year. Men and women around the world take to the highways and the "open air" is their kitchen. On the pages of this book, you'll discover how to buy, carry, prepare and store food while on tour. Discover the ins and outs with a "Baker's Dozen" of touring tips that are essential for successful bicycle adventuring. Whether you're going on a weekend ride, a weeklong tour or two years around the world, this handbook will help you learn the artistry of bicycling and cooking.

Strike Three! Take Your Base—The Brookfield Reader, Sterling, VA. To order this hardcover book, send $19.95 to Frosty Wooldridge by contacting him through his website. This poignant story is important reading for every teen who has ever experienced the loss of a parent from either death or divorce. This is the story of a boy losing his father and growing through his sense of pain and loss. It is the story of baseball, a game that was shared by both the boy and his father, and how baseball is much like life.

An Extreme Encounter: Antarctica— This book transports readers into the bowels of million-year-old glaciers, katabatic winds, to the tops of smoking volcanoes, scuba diving under the ice, intriguing people, death, outlaw activities and rare moments where the author meets penguins, whales, seals and Skua birds. Hang on to your seat belts. You're in for a wild ride where the bolt goes into the bottom of the world.

Bicycling Around the World: Tire Tracks for your Imagination—This book mesmerizes readers with animal stories that bring a smile to your face. It chills you with a once-in-a-lifetime ride in Antarctica where you'll meet a family of Emperor penguins. Along the way, you'll find out that you have to go without a mirror, sometimes, in order to see yourself. The greatest aspect of this book comes from—expectation. Not since *Miles from Nowhere* has a writer captured the Zen and Art of Bicycle Adventure as well as Wooldridge. Not only that, you may enjoy a final section: "Everything you need to know about long distance touring." He shows you "How to live the dream." You will possess the right bike, equipment, money and tools to ride into your own long-distance touring adventures. If you like bicycling, you'll go wild reading this book. If you don't like bicycling, you'll still go wild reading this book.

Motorcycle Adventure to Alaska: Into the Wind— Seldom does a book capture the fantasy and reality of an epic journey the magnitude of this book. Trevor and Dan resemble another duo rich in America's history of youthful explorers who get into all kinds of trouble—Tom Sawyer and Huckleberry Finn. They plied the Mississippi River, but Dan and his brother push their machines into a wild and savage land—Alaska.

Bicycling the Continental Divide: Slice of Heaven, Taste of Hell—This bicycle dream ride carries a bit of mountain man adventure. The author mixes hope with frustration, pain with courage and bicycling over the mountains. John Brown, a friend left behind to battle cancer, provides guts and heart for his two friends who ride into the teeth of nature's fury. Along the way, you'll laugh, cry and gain new appreciations while pondering the meaning of life.

Losing Your Best Friend: Vacancies of the Heart— This is one heck of a powerful book. It's a must read for anyone that has lost a friend or parent. It will give you answers that you may not have thought about. It will touch your heart and you will learn from their experiences. It also shows you what you can do if you suffer conflict with your friend's wife or girlfriend.

Rafting the Rolling Thunder— Fasten your raft-belts folks. You're in for the white-water rafting ride of your life. Wooldridge keeps readers on the edge of their seats on a wild excursion through the Grand Canyon.

Along the way, he offers you an outlaw-run by intrepid legend "High Water Harry," a man who makes a bet with the devil and nearly loses his life. The raft bucks beneath you as Harry crashes through Class V rapids. And the Grand Canyon Dish Fairies, well, they take you on separate rides of laughter and miles of smiles. Enjoy this untamed excursion on a river through time.

How to Deal with 21ˢᵗ Century Women: Co-Creating a Successful Relationship— The chapters on the nine key points for creating a successful long-term relationship are the best suggestions for anyone considering marriage. Every woman should read them along with her man. This is the first male relationship book that honors the male perspective and aims for sensible collaboration. I highly recommend this book for men and women.

How to Live a Life of Adventure: The Art of Exploring the World— If you endeavor to live like you mean it, to aspire to show up with passion and purpose, and take your being to maximum heart rate in mind and body—please allow Frosty to coach, inspire and guide you. *How to Live a Life of Adventure* will rock your body and soul, and enliven within you your belief and practice of living like you mean it—with passion and purpose.

America on the Brink: The Next Added 100 Million Americans— Electrifying reading! This is a veritable cannonade of a book. Wooldridge targets the people and institutions, from the president of the USA on down, who refuse to look at the consequences of population growth in the modern era. His focus is on the United States, but his range is the world. He fearlessly addresses issues that politicians fear to mention, such as the effects of mass immigration on our population future and social systems. He engages leaders to force population issues into our local and national political decisions.

Living Your Spectacular Life— This book entertains, inspires and motivates. What I liked most about it: Wooldridge offers other motivational writers in each chapter to give you new ideas on living a spectacular life. He wants you to succeed for your sake. If that means you enjoy a greater affinity to another writer, he gives you plenty of choices. He's got six concepts and six practices that provide you with personal courage, self-confidence and empowerment. He offers you dozens of ordinary men and women living spectacular lives in various pursuits from world travel to growing a garden. He kept me reading through every chapter.

Old Men Bicycling Across America: A Journey Beyond Old Age— This book is a ton of fun. Five gray-haired, bald and grizzled old guys get together around a campfire along with one of them a guitarist, and they sing and tell stories. If you can imagine that all of them had been married one, two and three times, well, their stories lifted into the treetops with outrageous laughter. More than that, they followed the Lewis & Clark Trail all the way to Bismarck, North Dakota on the northern tier bicycle route, the longest ride in America. This book will make you want to take the ride yourself.

Zen Between Two Bicycle Wheels: Eat, Pedal, Sleep—This book expands your spirit, body and imagination. Traveling with two 70-year-old, you can smell the campfires, the fresh ocean air, the seagulls, whales, sea lions, rugged Oregon Coastline, those enormous redwoods, San Francisco, Big Sur and dozens of other stops along the way. Highway 101 and 1 are as famous as Route 66 for bicyclists. Along the way, the author raises epiphanies about life, old age and the thrill of adventure. This book will keep you excited about the next page.

All books available at: 1 888 519 5121, www.amazon.com, www.barnesandnoble.com, also on Kindle.